D0802827

A PASSION
for MORE

ALSO BY SUSAN SHAPIRO BARASH

Sisters: Devoted or Divided

The Men Out There: A Woman's Little Black Book

*Second Wives: The Pitfalls and Rewards
of Marrying Widowers and Divorced Men*

*Reclaiming Ourselves:
How Women Dispel a Legacy of Bad Choices*

Inventing Savannah

*Mothers-in-Law and Daughters-in-Law:
Love, Hate, Rivalry, and Reconciliation*

A PASSION FOR MORE

wives reveal

the affairs that

make or break

their marriages

SUSAN SHAPIRO BARASH

berkeley hills books
berkeley california

Published by:
Berkeley Hills Books, PO Box 9877, Berkeley CA 94709

Copyright:
© 2001 Berkeley Hills Books

ISBN:
1-893163-24-5

Cover Design:
Elysium Design, San Francisco

Distributed to the trade by:
Publishers Group West

Back cover photograph:
® Alonzo Boldin

Acknowledgements

I am especially grateful to my three children, Jennie, Michael, and Elizabeth Ripps, for their patience and understanding. There is an indebtedness to others: my parents, Selma and Herbert L. Shapiro, my closest friends and extended family for listening. The professionals who contributed their thoughts to this book deserve a special mention: Dr. Jane Bloomgarden, Dr. Ronnie Burak, Dr. Donald Cohen, Dr. Jessica Lighter, and Dr. Bertram Slaff. My editor, Robert Dobbin at Berkeley Hills Books, warrants thanks for his extraordinary manner and his vision of the project. Also—Richard Grossinger of North Atlantic for his introduction, Robert Marcus, my attorney, for his excellent advice, Lori Ames, Barry Shils, Cynthia Vartan for their wisdom, and Dr. Robin Hirtz Meltzer for her insight.

A heartfelt thank you to the many women who came forward to tell their stories. They cannot be thanked by name because their names have been changed to insure confidentiality. But without these women, this book would not have been born.

Lastly, I thank my husband, Gary Barash, who patiently waits while I write, for his endless love.

All ye that be lovers call unto your remembrance the month of May, all as did Queen Guenever, for whom I make here a little mention, that while she lived she was a true lover, and, therefore, had a good end.

–Sir Thomas Malory
Camelot

Contents

Preface

During several casual lunches in Connecticut with women friends last fall, the conversation invariably seemed to turn to married women and their lovers. On another occasion, this time at a trendy New York restaurant, a friend spoke almost wistfully of her friend who was blithely conducting a torrid love affair with a married man while remaining happily married and deeply committed to mothering. "This guy," my lunch date reported, "makes every part of her life better, even marriage. Don't roll your eyes—that's a direct quote."

Soon after, I sat at a dinner party in the country and listened to yet another friend whisper a similar story, her admiration and envy obvious. And when I ran on the beach last summer, a jogging friend told me of her own "new" friend. It appeared that, wherever I turned, someone was having an extramarital affair. I was amazed, yet fascinated by the realization. Was it so prevalent? Did it affect married women everywhere? From all walks of life? How do they find the time and energy, I wondered—with children, a career, a demanding husband? How does an affair get started in the first place, and where do they meet afterwards without getting caught? And what about AIDS—aren't they concerned, even terrified? Was the sex so notably different from what they had with their husbands? Did they still do it with their husbands, the same day, the same night?

As a writer my curiosity was piqued; as a married woman I was overwhelmed. I wanted details, I needed reasons, I itched to hear the whole story and realized powerfully that many similarly situated women would want it too. This is why I pursued the interviews: to learn what women have to say about their secret liaisons, and to share this knowledge with other women.

Since my initial investigations, I have discovered there are many reasons why a married woman takes a lover. The rationales are diverse and often complex. A volatile subject from the start, this exploration has not only provided eye-opening insights into the female perspective on contemporary extramarital connections, but painted a sometimes startling portrait of how women in the early millennium are choosing to live their lives.

I began to read material on marriage and affairs. Much of the information seemed judgmental, moralistic, and sexist. Few books gave equal time to the idea of married women conducting affairs, focusing instead on the married man and his escapades. Even fewer addressed how women felt while in the midst of these relationships.

Because it was evident to me that many of my peers were indeed engaging in these triangles, I set out simply to hear their stories, leaving aside preconceived notions of right and wrong. All of us are aware that affairs have been in existence since the beginning of time. Throughout literature, mostly written by men (*Lady Chatterley's Lover, Madame Bovary, Anna Karenina*), infidelity is a recurrent theme. So it is the nature of these bondings today which is unprecedented, as is the attitude of the women who practice them. When Nancy Friday tells us in her book *Women on Top* that "our sexual lives are on a different course from earlier generations," we know it to be true.

I did not set out to re-create a Kinsey-type report, with its inevitable reams of questionable statistical data, nor to predict any emergent social trend or universal pattern. However, I do know as a certainty what is going on with a specific group of women today. Within a sphere of working-class, college-educated, middle- or upper-class married women, lovers are sought with a sense of entitlement. Women find them everywhere: in the workplace, at their children's school, the playground, a health club, or while an addition is being built onto their home. Taking lovers seem not a rite of passage, but something very possible at any time.

I recognized from the interviews I conducted that not every relationship results in a full-fledged, long-standing affair. As a professional in the field pointed out to me, women are seeking men outside of marriage in each instance, but not always to sustain a love affair. Friendship, anger, companionship, rebellion and pure sexual fulfillment must also be given their due. Women appear to appreciate the sense of control their self-initiated action produces; that is, if a man can do it and get away with it, so can a woman. The assumptions of a generation of married women have been shaken so that in their search for emotional satisfaction they have entered uncharted waters. Combine these factors with the narcissistic desire to battle growing old and less attractive, and an explosive potential for infidelity results.

The response to the project has been astonishing, from both interviewees and likely readership. It is that reaction which has impelled me to move forward, to share the fabric of *the other couple*, their intimacy and time together, to elicit and profile the feelings and thoughts it evokes in the women who experience the relationship. These women are the protagonists of this book; it is their stories that are told.

The women I spoke with fall between the ages of twenty-five and fifty-five. Some are childless, others have children. While they may bear little resemblance to each other in type, need and behavior, they share one common thread: the desire and willingness to go beyond monogamy, to break the marriage vows. These women may be urban or suburban or come from a small town anywhere in the United States. After putting out my initial feelers, numerous women contacted me, eager and enthusiastic, some almost driven, to re-count the most personal details of their attachment to their lovers. Each adventure is special and the disclosures go beyond anything I anticipated when I first embarked on this odyssey.

The level of interest and identification with the material on the part of women has been staggering, and convinced me that I had something engrossing to share. At the same time, the virtually uni-versal repudiation by men, especially husbands, has been equally dramatic. To say that not many husbands are pleased with the idea of their wife's lover floating about is understatement indeed.

I have followed as many leads as possible, honing in on how a woman's affinity with this other partner develops and how it has impacted her marriage. The results range from divorce to a strength-ened marriage, with the women's choice the most amazing part of the process. Some women feel they can sustain both—the lover and the husband—at once. These lovers provide a range of possibilities, from substituting for a part of a woman's marriage that is lacking to merely providing the best, kinkiest sex she's ever known. Often women talk about the childbearing, mothering, loneliness and inse-curity as ingredients that come into play. The interviews made me acutely aware that women are not alone in their needs and sensa-tions. These interviews are for women, not in derogation of women. They are a declaration that women today are not willing to accept this area of limitation in their lives. Bold female initiatives seem a natural outgrowth of these troubled times we live in, and those who seek the full-time lover strike the boldest pose of all.

What beguiles me about the inquiry is the increasing number of women who uphold the conventional image of wife and mother, yet are absorbed in unorthodox romances with men. The contour of each relationship sheds some light on what it is that modern women desire, and why sex, passion and love do not always come in one package. Women readily discuss their attraction to their lovers. We learn who these lovers are, where they first met, how often and where their secret rendezvous take place. They describe the erotic aspect of the affair, how they react to their husbands, juggle their lives and perhaps their children's lives too.

The double standard of fidelity still holds despite how far we've come. Beyond the sexual revolution, and the idealized working woman of the '80s and '90s, it still stands. Something meaningful and evolutionary is heard in these women's voices, in terms of women's ability to achieve their full potential at last. It is in the spirit of self-discovery and self-awareness that I offer tales of the other partner.

Introduction
by Dr. Ronnie Burak

છ૪૦

It is difficult to know whether more women are having affairs than in times past. However, one thing is very clear: women are now talking more openly about having extramarital relationships. The days of the *Scarlet Letter* are gone. Women today express their discontent with marriage more directly and expect much more out of their relationships with their husbands. Many women who are having affairs see themselves as having a right to be happier, and justify their pursuit of a relationship outside their marriage on that basis.

In the early days of my practice in rural Vermont, where people often said that we were ten years behind the times, I would hear my unhappily married women clients say that they felt guilty about being dissatisfied with their marriage. "After all," they would say, "my husband doesn't drink, or run around, or beat me, and he is a good provider and father. Shouldn't I be satisfied?" Now I hear women demanding, perhaps irrationally, to be happy in every aspect of their marriage, and what women seem to be asking for more than anything is intimacy and communication.

Marriage may be in peril, with the divorce rate at fifty percent in our country. The view of marriage as a sacred vow, for better or worse, lasting forever, has been replaced by insecurity and a woman's hope that her marriage will last longer than her friends' marriages have. Monogamy is threatened by this lack of certainty. Some women actually say that they carry on affairs in order to stay in their marriage. They talk about loving their husbands but wanting other kinds of experiences to make life fuller. They consider their husbands to be wonderful people but desire the newness and excitement that an affair provides. Instead of giving up a good thing, the stability and companionship of a marriage, they add to what they have with another relationship that offers romance and adventure. It is a question in this case of having one's cake and eating it too. Whether it works or not is an individual matter. One has to keep in mind that a marriage today could last up to fifty years. That's a long time, longer than a lifetime used to be. The wish to explore may very well have to do with such a projected length of the marriage.

Unfortunately, many women who are carrying on affairs are not as happy as they imagined they would be—even with having their cake and eating it too. They are often overwhelmed by anxiety and guilt and exhausted by trying to fit a secret relationship into their lives. Having an affair can be compared to being on drugs. There are the highs interspersed among the terrible lows. The lows, of course, come from the fear of being found out and the guilt about the pain it will cause their husbands and the other important people in their lives.

How things work out with a couple after an affair has come out into the open depends on how much real caring there is between the two, and how much both partners are willing to take responsibility for what happened. The situation is often workable if a husband doesn't see his wife's extramarital relationship as a reason to end the marriage, and he realizes that the affair may be the result rather than the cause of the problems in the marriage. Often I tell my clients that marriage is an unwritten contract. We have expectations in our head of what our marriage is supposed to be like. These expectations may be communicated very indirectly to our partner and may change over time without discussion between partners.

When a crisis occurs in a marriage it may be a way of unconsciously rewriting the unwritten contract. If a woman's needs are no longer being met, she may go elsewhere to find someone to meet those needs. Once the affair is made known, it may be an opportune time to talk about what has gone wrong in the marriage and how both partners can have their needs met better in the future. In this way the couple is rewriting their marriage contract with clarity and directness. The affair has become the catalyst to open communications for the first time. Had there been no affair, the couple might go on for years with their needs uncommunicated and therefore unmet.

Women who marry young seem particularly susceptible to having affairs. This may be a result of the fact that between eighteen and forty years of age there are incredible changes that take place in a woman's life. At forty she may be an entirely different person than she was at eighteen, and because of that her needs are entirely different. Often a woman who marries very young develops a strong dependence on her husband, and in leaning heavily on that man there is a price to pay.

The price of being taken care of is often being told what to do. As this woman grows, she no longer wants her husband controlling her life. If her husband can't hear her, she may act out her anger in what might be seen as adolescent rebellion. Often she looks for an affair with a man who will see her as a mature, adult woman. Rather than doing battle with a husband she regards as unbeatable, she escapes.

Women tell me that what they are missing most in their marriage is romance. They remember the days when they were dating their husbands, and when the time together was filled with romance and fun. They say that they felt 'special, beautiful, and appreciated. They want those feelings back.

One might say that comparing a lover to a husband is like comparing apples to oranges. Because of the illicit nature of the relationship and the lack of mutual responsibilities, a woman and her lover never engage in the more reality-oriented activities of a normal couple's life, such as paying bills, making grocery lists, doing laundry, cleaning the garage, dealing with irritable children, carpools, ball games, and homework. Each of the partners in the marriage moves in their own direction, and the duties seem to grow, building a wall between them. Soon it becomes difficult to break down the wall, and it may be easier to find intimacy with someone else.

A family is composed of units that are all screaming for attention. There is the family as a whole, the couple as a unit, the children as another unit, and each individual of the family as further subdivisions. Generally in a household where both the mother and father are working, most of the after-work and weekend time is given over to the children and the family as a whole. Some time may be given to the needs of the couple, but often this unit of the family gets the least nurturing and attention. Marriages and people are like cars—you can't keep running the vehicle, or the person, or the marriage without servicing it.

What a woman must understand when she compares her husband to her lover is that she is not comparing people but types of experiences. If a woman marries her lover he may turn from an apple into an orange. The big question is, Can a lover leave the fantasy world, do the mundane, and maintain his allure? It is important to remember that relationships with husbands also began in the fantasy world of dating and fun.

Many women feel that the best course of action is to work on keeping the romance in the marriage. Doing this takes a lot of time, energy, and willingness to let go of the old patterns and try new ones that at first may be more comfortable in a new relationship than an old one.

There are terrible marriages out there, but I wonder if marriage has become the scapegoat for our stressful, day-to-day, contemporary existence. The affair is a fantasyland that allows a woman to escape from her superwoman syndrome of trying to force too many things into her life. Now that women are out in the workaday world, men surround them at all levels. No longer do they have to wait for the plumber to be noticed. Men are more available to today's woman, and she is more tempted.

The concept of the family as the basic unit of our society may be in big trouble. I do believe, however, in Maslow's theory of the hierarchy of needs, which states that after food and shelter, humans search for security and belonging. Perhaps the shape and structure of the family will continue to change, but the need to strongly bond as a family group will remain.

It may be that as women marry older and are more experienced and more secure in themselves, the need for affairs will subside. Through the shared experiences of others, we as women may come to better understand our own needs and motivations and choose a path that will be the most growthful for ourselves and our families.

DR. RONNIE BURAK *has a Ph.D. in clinical psychology from the California School of Professional Psychology in Alameda, California. She currently practices in Jacksonville, Florida.*

empowering

affairs

1

Empowering Affairs

INTRODUCTION by DR. JESSICA LIGHTER

Dr. Jessica Lighter has a Ph.D. in psychology and has been in private practice for twenty-four years. The issues she most often deals with concern women: feminism, dual-career families, divorce, the effects of maternal employment on families.

Dr. Lighter's feeling is that, since there are more opportunities for women today on every level, women are looking for strategies to balance different aspects of their lives.

"Because women have joined the work force and have more autonomy over their own schedules and make their own money, real money, there is greater opportunity for them to associate with men as their peers and to pick and choose these men as their lovers.

"When a woman wants to meet a man for dinner and she is married, she is now able to pull it off. She has the money to treat for dinner and to pay for the hotel. Twenty-five years ago, this option was not possible. Currently, enough women move in and out of hotels and restaurants as part of their business lives that neither they nor the hotel clerks flinch when a woman registers for a room.

"Women have reached a level of parity, an equalization, of power status and economic remuneration. They have allowed themselves to make the same transgressions as their male counterparts of similar status. Such transgressions include extramarital affairs."

Dr. Lighter also recognizes a "stage-of-life and age perspective" in what transpires with married women and their lovers.

"Today the attitude of a woman in her late twenties or early thirties concerning an affair differs from that of a woman in her late thirties or early forties. The younger woman sees it as a possibility in a lifetime of marriage. These younger women were brought up at a time when women were encouraged to explore and discover their sexuality and received tacit acknowledgment from the media concerning their sexuality. What applies to women of any age, however, is the battle against a society where only a male's sexuality is celebrated."

The entitlement of women in the workplace and in terms of sexuality began in the sixties, but there are periods of greater and lesser progress in their liberation. "While the general research will tell you that married women are having affairs in greater numbers, I am not sure whether or not the trend will continue. A woman is now less chained to her marriage because of her monetary and emotional independence. Therefore when this woman remains in her marriage she is doing it out of choice rather than necessity. This in turn may provide for a stronger marriage.

"Sometimes there is the 'thunderbolt' that may walk into a woman's life. The thunderbolt is chemically and electrically shocking, someone who is unexpected, an attraction which shakes a woman up. Perhaps something has been missing for a woman to notice this man, perhaps not. The situation would be identical if the gender roles were reversed. The point is that the woman or man can make a conscious choice to follow the affair through. They have the power and thus the choice.

"The decision to have an affair is not guilt-free for women or men, particularly for women who are brought up to be caregivers and guilt-takers. For these women, a strong component of guilt or shame is often associated with the affair.

"Another phenomenon is the concept of 'experiencing' younger men, which is more common today than ever before. Younger men may aid in keeping a marriage intact, as younger women did for married men for so many years. The younger man becomes the object for the older woman as the younger woman has been historically for the older man. A man has traditionally traded his currency, i.e., wealth, power and status, for sexually nubile women. Today women are out there working and excelling and they are now trading in the very same currency for sexually nubile men. These women panic less when they are no longer young and beautiful. Women are presently entering the same sphere. They are attaining the same ability to feel great about themselves as a result of their achievements.

"These women are able to take their 'boy toys' as men took their mistresses, because a woman's currency has also increased. She too wants to keep intact her home and family. Therefore her lover may never reach the level where he is a threat to her marriage.

"What we are witnessing is a 'short-term lease' view of young, sexual men, or men in general, instigated by women. Why upset the whole family when you can lease him, short or long term, for whatever need he fulfills? And so women are coming into their own, adapting these relationships to suit their requirements as men have done throughout the generations."

The question of why certain women act out and others do not vis-à-vis lovers is case-by-case as it is for men, according to Dr. Lighter.

"There is no one answer for so complex an issue. Each person brings her own creativity and set of issues to the situation.

"As we start the new millennium, our society questions whether marriage is necessary to have children, whether men have to be the larger wage earners in a marriage or relationship, whether mothers have to be under forty to begin a family.

"Whether or not to have an affair becomes an issue to consider along with the other changing issues of our time."

CR&O

Sarah

A forty-five-year-old woman, Sarah, spoke in a throaty, confident voice about her experiences with her lovers. What was most striking was her ability to analyze her own sexuality and the results she expected from these relationships.

It was obvious from meeting Sarah that she has a heightened self-awareness and is in touch with her specific needs. Her upbringing was not conventional and she feels it is that exposure that allows her to proceed as she does.

She described her first marriage as "unusual."

"My husband was older by a substantial number of years. After a time I began to grow as a person and he began to feel insecure that I'd leave him for a younger man. He began to belittle me in many areas and made me feel worthless and inept in every aspect of my life. He enjoyed being a Pygmalion, educating me, introducing me to a higher quality of life, a material life."

The trouble came when Sarah began to develop on her own. By that time they had a child. She portrays herself as fairly desperate. When she was in her late twenties, he pulled the ropes tighter and tighter. If she went out with friends or to work, he would check on her to see that she was at the place she claimed to be.

Although she was not involved with anyone else, her husband did not believe it. Soon after, they became divorced, an unexpectedly benign episode.

"The divorce was easy because I made the decision to get free from him, thinking it was more important than any material thing I might have to fight for."

When asked how she felt about men during this interval, Sarah defined her needs.

"I was looking to other men for affirmation that I was still an attractive human being. I was very intimidated by men. At the end, we did not get divorced right away but split up physically. My husband moved away and I got involved with someone. It was not a love-seeking relationship but an affirmation of my worth. I wanted to feel beautiful, desired, strong, intelligent. I had lost all that."

She considered herself still married, although separated, and it was at this juncture that she began to take on lovers. She had two lovers at the same time, which she described as "predominantly physical relationships."

"Both men were single, and neither exerted the same amount of power over me as my husband did and it was a relief. I alternated one week per guy. It was a wetting of my toes. I was terrorized by the whole aspect. I felt a little tense, a sense of concern about seeing these men while I was still married, but the physical separation helped."

When asked to tell us a little about these lovers, Sarah characterized her first one as a "gymnast."

"He was very young and comfortable with his body, very relaxed; from a completely different world. I like it that way. We did it in very weird positions and I had never done that. My husband had not been relaxed about his body and so I wasn't relaxed about mine. The first time I was with my gymnast, I was so powdered and perfumed and clean he asked me to leave off the cologne in the future. It was a whole new experience in being natural, a different level of intimacy. It made me happy, comfortable with my own body. I began to recognize that I was not a misfit; there was nothing hideously wrong. I learned that by society's standards I had a good body. Ultimately, when it ended, we became friends."

In reflecting on today, Sarah explains that she continues to need affirmation from men.

"It has to do with chronological age more than anything else. Today my marriage, my second marriage, is successful, and while I don't wish to jeopardize anything, I still have these lovers. It's as if the logical part of my brain says it's a great marriage, and the insecure side sees time running out—the time to still look good, the fact that now is the best I'm ever going to be physically. Will it be maintained? I better act fast. I'm getting older and I want to still hold on."

It is for these reasons that Sarah sustains her lovers of the present, men she claims play no part in her life except for the need they fill—a temporary, unemotional, physical relationship. She has had two lovers in her present marriage but not simultaneously, as during her first marriage. "Neither has impacted me emotionally or long term. I think of it as a zipless fuck."

The lovers come from a part of the population she has little to do with—single, unencumbered, from very unique backgrounds.

"I meet these lovers anywhere. Once you are open toward meeting someone it's a matter of body language. Since I'm looking for someone from another walk of life, I tend to meet them anyplace, on line to go to a movie, in a taxi where the cab driver can be attractive, and so it begins. Once the initial contact has occurred, I usually go to their place for our interludes. But once I went to a motel with a much younger man and I was so nervous. I paid because he had no money and I wanted us to be somewhere half-decent. Anyway, I learned that hotels have special day rates. Neither of us knew; I had never gone to a hotel and he was too young and poor.

"They are younger men, one twenty-eight years old and the other thirty. I see it as if they've fallen in and fallen out. It. may seem shocking to you that someone youthful could be interested in me, and yet it is the most exciting thing in my life, the fact that they could be interested."

Her attitude toward men today, she says, is one in which she feels more power, a result of the present marriage.

"My husband has allowed me to go out and explore my own self. He's the best from a physical aspect. Yet I want someone very exciting, who can turn me on right away, get my underpants wet immediately rather than the tried and true. Sex with my husband is ultimately better than with these young men—that's the irony. It's just not as exciting initially.

"Although it feels somewhat separate, like it's not really me, I want to pursue these men. I am basically modest, externally flamboyant but internally shy. For me there is no such thing as a casual relationship. But because I'm so amazed by the interest of a twenty-eight-year-old man, I follow it through. What's in it for me? Maybe what it is—a physical encounter, nothing more. Yet it's not always a fulfilling encounter. The first time I was with one of my latest lovers, I had to laugh. I was unfulfilled sexually. I had to go home to my husband for an orgasm. So while the admiration is important, I had to ask myself if it would be sufficient without the sexual encounter. My husband is more satisfactory, a better lover. I think it's the established knowledge of what it is I enjoy. I'm a little inhibited and I can't tell a stranger what will turn me on. I can't open up. It's as if I'm going into it handicapped, as opposed to the comfort and recognition in a sexual relationship within the marriage. It's strange. One friend described a lover as someone with whom you rarely share an orgasm. Instead you worry if your legs are shaved. You are too insecure, not relaxed enough to enjoy it. In other words, are you moaning too loud or too low? Are you wishing for it too much?"

So although Sarah is attached to her husband, she is also locked into the lure of the lover. When asked if she appreciates her husband more after her affairs have ended, she replied: "Yes, but it might not stop me from doing it again. I find it's the pressure from society of trying to feel youthful all the time. I'm not eager to get involved with anyone who would endanger my existence as it presently is. That is, nothing emotional. I can't live with an emotional entanglement. I have a tendency, as most women do, to be more sentimental than men. I know that a dependency would form. I'd be waiting for the phone to ring to the point where it would exclude other parts of my life. I don't want to get hooked on another person. I'm fortunate. I choose lovers who won't put me in that position. I purposely choose them."

Sarah is convinced that if her husband knew about her affairs he would be "incensed." While not positive it would end her marriage, it would certainly cause a "major rift." On the other hand, Sarah does not believe that she would be alarmed to learn that her husband was having an affair.

"If you take the history of marriage and what it historically is supposed to mean and compare it with today's longevity, it's almost unnatural. Who can live with the same person for forty years? Within that time frame I believe people are going to be attracted to someone else, but there are other aspects of marriage besides sex. That's what holds it together."

The interesting thing here, psychologically speaking, is the split that Sarah describes, almost as if two different people exist within her. She separates herself, her worlds and functions, without much overlap. This splitting mechanism allows her to relate to each of the worlds she has constructed effectively.

Sarah is preoccupied with herself in a way that makes her desirability and attractiveness her top priority. Anything–any person, any experience that feeds her feelings of attractiveness–is compelling to her. In our society, with its emphasis on eternal youth and beauty, a woman's self-esteem gets connected to these values. In this instance, it seems that Sarah can only maintain her opinion of herself through these various relationships.

Her directness is unique, as is her unromanticized view of what she desires. Sarah is into the basics; many of her needs are sexualized but her candor enables her to achieve these needs. Her attitude is one of honesty, and the affection she seeks is honestly in terms of sex.

CB&C

Alice

Alice was twenty-two years old when she married Gregory and moved to northern California, where she has lived ever since. Her childhood, shared with one brother, was normal until she was sixteen and her parents divorced. She then found herself alone and working full-time while she took courses at a local college in the evenings. Eventually, after working in hospitals, waitressing and doing secretarial work, she quit college and continued taking courses on and off. When asked what sort of men she dated before she met Gregory, she described them as parodies of her father. She described herself as "blatantly promiscuous" before she got married. The reason Alice dated men like her father was to "win as an adult with the tool of sex." She then told us that her father had always been distant and uninterested in her because she was a girl.

Alice met Gregory through a mutual friend. She characterizes their courtship as nonexistent: "We went out on a Saturday and the next Thursday we moved in together and three weeks later we were married."

They have been married for thirteen years, and the marriage evolved with Gregory as a father figure. Alice considered Gregory the "father of my dreams."

"Gregory was the father initially. The thought that Gregory was pleased that I enjoyed school was wonderful. We could talk about the meaning of life. My husband was the first person in my life to say that I was attractive and smart. He was a Svengali for me. I began to try things I'd never done before with the emotional and financial freedom he provided. And then three years ago I no longer needed a father but a friend, partner, lover. Now I needed someone exciting and fun."

The adjustment to the change, to these new roles necessary for Alice to move forward, proved difficult. During this period of turmoil Alice admits a new feeling toward men put her in a state of utter confusion. Unexpectedly, she found herself attracted to another man, the antithesis of Gregory in almost every respect. Would such an event have taken place if her own head had been in another place—if she hadn't wanted Gregory to be more fun, to no longer father her?

"There was a nineteen-year-old exchange student who had come to live with us that summer. I was very attracted to him; it was frightening. He proved the young lover I wasn't ready for when I was young. I'd never felt attracted to anyone besides Gregory, ever. Gregory is my best friend. Then I had these strong sexual feelings for this young man. I'd never cared before, not for sex or anything. I'd never desired anyone. I began to give him driving lessons and in the car... we'd be necking in the back of the car. I looked forward to this part of my day; I'd be thinking about it all day long, fantasizing about the night and how it would be. I only wanted to be with this student. I'd return from these driving lessons craving sex. Actually the sex was better between my husband and me than it had been in a long time as a result. My husband benefited from my attraction to another man. This kid would get me riled up. I felt more like a sexual being than I'd felt in years, more desirable, and more satisfying and satisfied. I guess Gregory and I had fallen into a pattern that a lot of married couples do with young children, caught up in our roles as providers and parents, but not as sexual beings. So someone else made me feel I was a sexual being and the outlet was my husband, who I'm so comfortable with. But mixed with it were guilt and frustration, my own confusion.

"The exchange student and I spent time in the house together too. We were there all day, the kids at school, Gregory at work. Or if Gregory took the kids to the store, we'd be alone together, like teenagers when their parents left the house, those moments alone.

"During this time period I was obsessed with how I looked, something I hadn't thought about in a long while. I gave careful attention to what I wore with this man and I bought Oil of Olay. I was very conscious of looking older, of no longer looking healthy. Suddenly this really bothered me. He was a symbol, a teenager. And I only wanted to do whatever he wanted. It was like being eighteen again. And then at the dinner table with my husband and the children there, he'd be mouthing across the table, 'I want you.' It was a heady experience. I was able to be eighteen again. I told Gregory I was attracted, that I felt all these things. He said, 'I trust you; it's just a phase.' He didn't understand."

Alice's confiding in her husband was a cry for help. She pursued the relationship with the exchange student until his visit ended. He was to return to Europe and Alice took him to the airport.

"He told me he had the money to buy another ticket. I almost went. I almost left my husband and children. I wanted to leave them. I wanted a life of sex, fantasy, free of obligations and responsibility."

She described the event as if it were happening to another person, a sensation she has not experienced before or since. After the student left, Alice felt very confused.

"I felt like I was married to an old man. I felt as if the one chance at being carefree and young was gone and I never had it before and would never have it again. I almost left my husband. Then I talked a lot with Gregory and we both learned that we needed our relationship to change."

For Alice, her sex/love interest in a young man was a signal there was trouble within the marriage. Although not always the case, it was a symptom of her problem.

"We needed to be equal partners in marriage. I realized that we needed to develop fun things to do together. Gregory needed to be more adventurous on his own."

When asked about her feelings today toward the other partner, Alice replied that the relationship existed long-distance for a time after the student left.

"At first we called and wrote each other, so things continued for months long-distance. Initially after he left I was confused and longing for the experience. Then, gradually, resignation set in. I began to realize that this is what I have—and should accept it. A caring husband and children, a network of close friends. I'm very fortunate. I look back and realize this is a source of feelings of guilt and also necessary transition for me to go on to the next stage of my marriage."

While she sees the experience as a service to her marriage, she does wish that the change might have happened without it.

"I have a pit in my stomach whenever I think about it. The other day my husband drove down the road, we were in the car together, where we'd first parked, and I couldn't stand it, to drive there. I suffer with it. But I also realize I grew from it. I was always a good girl, a nice girl. I came from a good family, prim and proper. I always went to church. Then my parents divorced and I was thrown to the winds and became promiscuous. Then I got married to Gregory and was good again. Then it came again and happened, this young student, when I had a good life. It's difficult to think about… I felt weak and bad."

In sharing her experience with close women friends, Alice told us that she evoked two very different reactions.

"My closest friend was also having a difficult time in her own marriage and she found it almost exciting. Without enabling her to talk about her own feelings, she was able to enjoy my situation. My other friend was the opposite. She kept saying, 'Why is this happening? Think about it." '

While Alice's was not a long-standing affair, her husband was apprised of the entire episode in bits and pieces once the student was gone.

"He knows what transpired. It took a long time for it to all come out and we had to work through it. Most of the time I can let go of the guilt and shame. He's very affirming. Sometimes we'll be together and I'll see a cute guy and I'll comment and he'll joke and say, 'Oh, no, he's too old, you need someone about nineteen or twenty.' My husband's message is that he loves me in spite of it."

When examining Alice's brief interlude with her lover, it can be seen as a positive incident, one that brought forth a better understanding of Alice's requirements and a reevaluation of what is important to her. Alice's primary interest and connection were to her husband—as if her preoccupation with the young student was beneficial only insofar as it furthered her relationship with her husband. The student was the tool for developing different emotional levels in the marriage. Also, her relationship with the student had to do with her reaction toward her father and could be seen as an attempt to repair the hurt and damage she had suffered at his hands.

CRING

Honey

Honey is forty-one years old and lives in a suburb in the Northeast, having spent her childhood in California and New York. When she was growing up her parents' marriage was intact. Although she describes her childhood as neither happy nor unhappy, it was characterized by "peaks and valleys" precipitated by her father's penchant for gambling. Although her childhood resembled that of children in the average nuclear family, Honey suffered her father's disappointments.

She was first married when she was twenty-two, a marriage she describes as "terrible." Her husband, who was five years older, was an alcoholic, and "I had to get out." Once she was divorced, she began to date frequently and was married again in a year's time. Her present husband is eight years older and they have two children, a year apart. When asked about her marriage, Honey described it as "excellent—although that wasn't always the case."

From the start of Honey's interview she was articulate about herself and clearly in touch with her feelings about her lover relationship.

"What taxed the marriage for me was having two children so close together and giving up my career to raise them. I felt it was depressing and alienating. And our marriage needed mending. There wasn't enough communication; we needed serious revision in terms of how we treated each other. After six years of being married I began an affair, which had enormous repercussions. It was an intense affair that I eventually ended. I carried the secret of that affair with me for ages. I am the type of person who would never have actively arranged an affair, but someone seduced me. A workman came to do a big job on our house, every day, day in, day out. I got to know him. I was lonely, vulnerable, and he was there. He almost became a part of the family, this stranger who would come and go. He knew how to seduce me and I eventually learned that it was a way of life for him. He'd go from house to house, affair to affair, unhappily married himself. He was from a completely different background, and that was part of the attraction, but neither ethnicity nor education was critical. It was his age—a father figure, fifteen years older than I, that was significant.

"We met in the summer. He came to talk about the job with my husband and initially I had no reaction to him. Then as the job got going, two months into it, I was getting to know him. He started to come on to me. At first I resisted, then he wore me down. I was attracted to him, absolutely.

"We were in the house together having sex and at hotels. Afterwards I felt horrible about doing it in the house, not hotels. The sex was good, very different. We had more oral sex than in my marriage and the sex itself lasted longer, the time devoted to turning each other on. The whole experience made me more sexual and that came out in the marriage too. In other words, I used the sex with him to aid sex with my husband. Only later, once the affair was over, did I feel guilty about anything. While it was going on I was simply obsessed. I felt sexier than ever in my life. This feeling prevailed not only with my lover but with any man I'd come across. The affair awakened me sexually. I felt more uninhibited with my lover than with my husband. We had anal sex. He was a superb lover. I could have multiple orgasms with him, which wasn't happening in my marriage at that time."

Honey explained that her lover and her husband had an interaction because of the construction on the house, and that she considered her lover's morals to be "nonexistent."

"For several months I slept with him, always during the day. Meanwhile, he paid for everything, hotels, meals. He really courted me. He thought I was special. But there he was treating me so well, his manners were impeccable, while he took my husband's money and was screwing me. I was tense whenever they spoke, the two men. I knew he'd managed these affairs before with 'the wife' but I still got nervous that he'd say something. My husband didn't notice anything. I mean my whole world had changed, I was feeling schizophrenic and my husband didn't even notice our sex was changed. I thought I was wearing a scarlet A. I couldn't believe he didn't pick up on anything. It made me question his feelings about me, and mine toward him. Yet he would never have had an affair."

Describing how often she and her lover had sex, Honey tells us that she was "obsessed" with him when he wasn't around, although they were together a few days a week.

"I lost an incredible amount of weight and concentrated more on my looks. I was happy for a brief time, then I quickly became bored. It was strictly sexual, the relationship. There was an excitement in the breaking of the rules, but it was emotionless, and that is why I became bored. Still, I needed the male attention he gave to me, something my husband wasn't giving at that time. He was too self-involved and preoccupied with work."

The affair began to alter Honey's self-esteem once she "wanted out." Then she was frightened.

"I didn't want to offend him. He could have ruined my life. I felt trapped, he had so much on me. Then what happened was that his son, who worked on the crew, found out and had a big fight with his father. So my lover admitted we had to cool it until he could put his family back in order. Ironically, although I wanted to end it, I then had tremendous problems with the rejection. I became depressed and I craved him, I really wanted him. I went into a deep depression, I was obsessed with him. Finally I got into therapy and my doctor said it had to do with my childhood and the rejection of my father. The therapy helped. Then my lover wanted to come back and I had to slam the door in his face many times until he finally got the point. The last time I saw him was a year or two after the affair was over. He actually stopped by because he was doing some work in the neighborhood, and I was very rude to him. In fact, my husband said to me that I behaved poorly, but I couldn't believe he'd dare show up."

Asked if she'd ever been concerned with getting caught while it was happening, Honey replied, "I wasn't afraid of getting caught at hotels. Only sometimes in the car, riding home, I'd worry. We would take separate cars then meet, but when we drove part of the way together, I'd worry. We had special restaurants, special places that we shared. That was nice. We drove far to these restaurants, so we avoided anyone we knew. I wasn't worried with the hotels, because I didn't believe anyone I knew would go there. Only one friend knew of my affair and unfortunately she was supportive. She was not a not a judgmental person, and besides, she did it also. The result was that she condoned it.

"I felt divided, like I was living two different lives, which brought out the good and the bad. Sometimes it helped me to have a secret, sometimes it was overwhelming. I was lucky–during my affair I didn't contract any disease, and I didn't get pregnant. The long-term effects were nil. It was a true affair, an interlude, brief, but all-encompassing. It had a profound effect on me. It changed my life, and my husband's. The dust didn't settle for a long time after my husband found out."

Honey's spouse learned of her affair when he accused her of having a relationship with another man.

"I carried the secret with me and the guilt was enormous. He was ready to hear it or he would not have asked. But his reaction was so intense, so negative, filled with pain and confusion. It nearly tore our marriage apart. Although I was relieved on my part because I confessed, the effect on the marriage was terrific, more than the affair had ever been while I kept quiet. I'd been advised professionally not to tell for the very reason that it could create such havoc. I love my husband very much. I loved him when the affair was going on.

"Once he found out my husband stopped trusting me and I thought our marriage would end. Then our sex became incredible because he knew that it was only the sex that differed in the affair; there was no love. And he wanted me to be happy in bed. We worked on being honest and attentive like never before. Now my marriage is sensational, growing on every level. Despite the highs and fun of the affair, I don't know that I'd risk it again. The man I was attracted to quite recently, the one my husband asked about, was a colleague. He is ten years younger, a departure for me. I resisted having an affair because of my experience with my former lover. So, indirectly, my one affair helped me to not begin another relationship. I felt I paid a high price but my marriage could not have improved without it. It helped in terms of self-exploration."

At the end it sounds as if Honey has achieved an intellectual rationalization for her relationship with the other man, as if she were never completely in touch with her guilt and anxiety. Hence the confession/absolution syndrome with her husband. The affair seems to have resulted from low self-esteem, a feeling she experienced post-childbirth. Although she did not see this man as a father figure, she needed a "father" to offset the demands of mothering. Her lover nurtured her like a father would, the ideal father that she never had; thus she gravitated toward an older man to support her in a fatherly way. In telling her husband everything, she repented as a gambler repents, and became good again. The bad girl/good girl syndrome parallels the bad gambler/good gambler syndrome.

Honey was capable of articulating the stages with her lover. The relationship was divided into: 1) the neutral period, when they first met and there were no signs of intention; 2) the surprise and seduction; 3) the intimacy that formed, characterized by obsession; 4) the final state: guilt and anxiety followed by confession and absolution.

CRED

Anamarie

At the age of thirty-eight, Anamarie works for a large firm and met her lover through a business meeting. Since then, the two have been exchanging love letters via email. Although they have not met since then, Anamarie views this affair as all-consuming.

"I have been having a virtual affair for eighteen months, "Anamarie tells us. "I met my lover last spring and we write each other emails about six times a day. I am always on the computer and I will drop anything I'm doing when I get his email. People have commented on the change in my work habits but no one knows what is going on. At home, on weekends, I use my daughter's computer to email my lover. My husband is absolutely clueless, and I see no reason why he would find out. If my marriage had any intimacy, I would not be involved with another man. My one friend who is my confidante keeps telling me that this is bogus, and that you can't really know anyone by email. I disagree. We even have virtual sex by email. We also are quite romantic at times and other times we buoy each other through our miserable marriages and demanding children. Whatever the other needs, we give it.

"There is something so pure and dependable about this affair that I'm not sure I can be without my lover. From the moment I met him, I felt something, but this constant email has made it much deeper and much more meaningful. Having met my lover once, I know he is my type and I love his looks. He reminds me of the person I always thought I'd meet one day, but I was never lucky enough, not at the right time, anyway. I do wish that we could meet sometimes, but it seems too risky. He is more worried about it than I am and I have to respect this. I don't know if it would change anything anyway–I feel that I've come to know him really well by this method. We also talk on the phone sometimes, but not anywhere near the amount that we email. I bought a cell phone once I met him, because I wanted him to be able to reach me at any time. After a long day at work and a sleepless night in my house, I will sneak off and call him. He also has a wife and kids. There's no question that this is not going anywhere.

"I sometimes wonder what I would do without this relationship. My lover advises me on work-related stuff, he knows about my kids, my dogs. And I know about his life. Neither of us is happily married, but we both feel there is too much at risk to get divorces. He would find it financially draining, and claims his wife would make life more miserable if he asked for a divorce. I know on my end that I won't have my lover once I am divorced, so I don't know if I'll do it so fast. On the other hand, my lover has shown me a whole world that exists without my husband. The chance to be open and honest with a man, to really talk about your feelings is very special. I have never been this close to anyone. I believe that he returns my feelings, although he isn't half as emotional as I am.

"There were times in the beginning of the affair when I was very frustrated because my lover and I did not see each other. I had visions of going to a hotel and having wild sex. But this has not materialized, and either he's convinced me that our cyberspace affair works or I've convinced myself. I have a completely different take on the work week because at work I really get to communicate with him, via email. If I thought he would be divorced one day, my entire life would be changed. And at that point, I would give up the email and go straight for the physical parts. The emotional parts are already there, for sure.

"What is so amazing is how deeply in love I feel I am with him. I think about him all the time and I love his manner. He is so unlike my husband—and so impressive. I know his life is a mess, and that there are parts of it that would be hard to handle, but I would be willing. About six months ago, I felt I was in a holding pattern with him and I told him so. I was upset and I complained. He explained that this is how it is for now and that may be it will be different in the future, if I can hang in. I made the decision to wait, because the idea of not having his emails and his cell phone calls is too depressing. He is really at the center of my life. I don't feel guilty when it comes to my husband at all, and my mothering skills are even better, because I'm happier since my lover came into my life."

While Anamarie did not fall in love with her lover through the internet, it is the primary vehicle of communication for the affair. One wonders how much the lover fills a void in Anamarie's life, how much of what she feels is infatuation and how much of it is real. A relationship without touch or sex or eye-to-eye contact has to be missing something. Yet the idea that people can open up by email and become intimate on this level is fascinating and futuristic. The 'holding pattern' which Anamarie describes makes sense, because her affair exists without any plans at all—not even a dinner date a week hence. The fact that she is willing to remain in the status quo reveals how much she depends upon the relationship, virtual or not.

CB80

Melanie

Melanie comes from a small town in Ohio, grew up in a "conventional family" and has been working in a midsize city since the early eighties. She met a man when they were both working in the telecommunications industry and immediately married. She found her husband, Frank, to be "remote" and "inattentive." Once they had a child and her intense career ended, Melanie no longer cared so much that Frank was a "shadow husband."

"Once our second child was born, Frank got a job in North Carolina and we all moved. I was very unhappy by then, bored and stuck at home with the kids. And being in a new place made it even worse. I couldn't get through to Frank about my feelings. He acted as if my problems didn't exist. I begged to go back to work and get help for the kids. It was what I really wanted.

"One day when I couldn't stand it anymore, I got a sitter and went to an employment agency to get a job in the computer industry and re-enter the workplace. I knew it was my only salvation. Within a week I had secured the services of a housekeeper and had landed a good job. With Frank protesting like crazy, I went back to work."

It was at that point that Melanie met her lover.

"My boss at the new job was an attractive older man. He was married and quite well respected at work. He always complimented me on my dress, my looks, any work I did for him. I was attracted to him as well. But we were both married and he was older. He never attempted anything else but it was in the air, I sensed it continually.

"I was content to leave the relationship as a friendship; I knew it was safer. Then one day he called me into his office and said there was a convention coming up and that I had to go. He said I should make arrangements to be away for several days and that other people from work would be attending. Needless to say, Frank did not want me to go. He was vehement about it. I told him it was important for my career and that I had no choice.

"At the convention we had drinks, my boss and I. Then we ended up going to bed together. This was the beginning of a long-standing affair. It was something that lasted for several years and was a very meaningful part of my life. We would meet in motels once a week and in his house in the summer when his family was on vacation. We tried to go to as many business conventions and on as many business trips as possible. The effort to be together was enormous and I would do anything to accomplish it."

The relationship with her lover was about sex and companionship.

"He was attentive and cared about me. He listened to me. I really needed that. I was attracted to him, and I liked the way he treated me. He listened to everything I had to say and bought me gifts and made me feel special. Had I not had the affair, I might not have stayed in my marriage. Without the escape of the affair and the pleasure it gave me, I could not have tolerated life with my husband."

Apparently Frank suspected the relationship from the start but did not ask for any details.

"He said nothing for a long while and then finally, after years, he confronted me. I told him I was seeing a man who lavished attention upon me and made me feel good. I explained that I intended to continue the affair until he was able to start treating me better. I didn't want to leave the marriage for my lover but I really wanted more from the primary relationship. I wasn't willing to give up my lover if Frank was going to treat me as he had been treating me. I stood my ground." Frank and Melanie began therapy, which she was happy to do.

"I guess I did want Frank and the marriage on some level. I wasn't able to face how much until years had gone by and I'd been with another man for that period. By the time he said something, I was ready to face the marriage. I guess the timing worked in our favor because my lover was transferred to another city just then. When Frank finally got wise he realized it was time he appreciated me and the children. In a strange way, our entire family has benefited from the experience."

Melanie's affair ended naturally when her lover was removed by distance and her therapy improved her relationship with her husband.

"In a way it was the best thing that ever could have happened to me in terms of the marriage. Today Frank and I are on the right track and my lover enriched my life at a point when I needed it."

The love affair for Melanie began because of poor marital relations. She experienced her husband being hardly there for her. Melanie ended up orchestrating an affair as a means to avoid the emptiness she experienced in the marriage. She became involved with a man who she realized would be attentive and was interesting to her. Only when there was a confrontation did she have to make a decision. Melanie was able to recommit to the marriage and force her husband to face the issues in it.

附 80

Patricia

Patricia, at the age of thirty-seven, lives in South Carolina, in the same area where she grew up. Her childhood was "totally normal and happy." Patricia's days were filled with riding lessons, dance lessons and school. She was very popular in high school and married her high school sweetheart. Today she is divorced from her husband and works full-time at a restaurant.

"I was married at the age of eighteen. I married my boyfriend, who had been a football player; I had been a cheerleader. We were a noticeable couple and we completed the picture by getting married. The marriage lasted over ten years and we had two children."

Patricia describes the marriage as "fine at the start" but as time went on she realized she was making compromises to be there. "I began to know I was sticking it out. We had children and we'd been together for so long. He was only nineteen when we married, so both of us had been too young, really. Because we didn't have children right away I thought the relationship was working. Then my husband got involved with someone else, someone we all knew. I was devastated. Everyone heard about it in the place where we lived. It was talked about and I realized that. Until then I'd never looked at another man. I'd stayed true to the marriage.

"As soon as I knew what was going on, I got involved with someone I'd known through my husband. He was my husband's friend and my friend from high school. He and my husband played sports together; they'd been close. Because we were friends before we became lovers, we were emotionally involved. I hesitated to get involved physically because I didn't want to hurt the friendship. And I'd lost all trust in my husband so how was I sure I could trust this man? I began to think, within my limited experience, that it was men in general and I was afraid."

Once Patricia's relationship with her lover had become a physical and emotional attachment, she was ready to see the marriage end.

"My husband left at that point and I was okay about it. I realized that this setup was better than the marriage in many ways. My lover had never been seriously involved with anyone else and he was free to be with me. I would say the sex was much better than in the marriage. He was more available for me and we were very tight. The sex means so much emotionally and he is more attentive and caring. From the start of our getting together we had sex all the time. And while I worried about risking the friendship for sex it simply made everything work together. I made the commitment to my lover because I knew I'd never go back to my husband once he did what he did. The lover relationship made me realize I could have something else."

Patricia is still in touch with her husband because of the children.

"It's been difficult, having to see him. The kids live with me, though, and have a strong attachment to this guy. He's like a big kid himself and loves to do things with them. He's a father to them, really. Although my ex-husband lives nearby, the children are with me. We are a family unit that works well. But I never wanted children with this man, not at any point in the relationship. Part of the consideration was financial and part of it was that I did not want to be tied down again. Why start all over? I thought. My kids are growing up and getting independent.

"By the time I got into the relationship with my lover, I knew what I wanted. I was older and I understood what it was to have children and to work full-time. He has never demanded that we have children so it's been fine. We have been together for a long time."

Recently, Patricia and her lover were married.

"Now that I'm settled in with this guy, I can say that it was probably the wrong option to be married at eighteen to a man the same age, almost. I was someone who could have pursued a career in acting or modeling. Those chances slipped by, if they existed at all, with the choice I made. So I'm relieved that my husband is gone, in a way, because I would not have done what he did. I wouldn't have made the break. The relationship which came as a result of my husband's affair is a much better one for me.

"Today I'm pleased that I chose this man and I'm very content. Then I think that maybe I don't have the energy to go elsewhere—that could be part of it. I'm relieved that someone treats me as he does after my first marriage. And I ask myself, are any men worth it? None of them seem to be. To go on to the next one and hope for something more seems like a lot of energy for nothing.

"Besides, with no other kids, maybe I could go after the career I never had. I was trapped for so long, in a small town with young children and a bad marriage. Now I could go out and seek it. The time is still there and I know he would let me. That's the difference."

Patricia married young out of naivete, not to escape her home life. What happened next was that she realized her mistake, and the marriage began to falter. When her husband took on a lover, Patricia became disillusioned and sought one for herself. Fortunately this lover was what Patricia dreamed of emotionally and physically. She felt cared for by him and was able to develop this into a long-term commitment.

Cஐஐ

Kristen

Kristen, who was born and raised in a "working-class" Rhode Island family, is twenty-eight years old and led a "happy, sheltered" childhood. Married at twenty-one for the first time, she remained married almost two years. She was married for the second time at twenty-five. Neither marriage produced children.

"My first marriage was to someone who was my age. We both were very young and while I was ready for marriage, I don't think that he was. For the most part, though, I never looked at other men; they were nonexistent. Toward the end of the marriage I met a guy who was pretty special. I was in Europe because my husband was in the military. And we'd been having some communication problems. I went to a club with some girlfriends and met a guy from New York. He was also in the military and I thought he was a friendly guy. He was not overly flirtatious when we first met. We spoke for an hour after the club closed and then I kept running into him, which I decided must mean something."

Kristen "purposely returned" to the States soon after she met this man, in order to "avoid a relationship."

"But I called him whenever my husband and I were fighting, and then this man came back home. Basically he followed me. By then I was hooked emotionally and he stayed in the States for several months. That was when we began our affair. When he left to go back to work abroad, our relationship continued. I followed him this time, back to Austria. My husband almost found out. It was close. Only later on did I learn that my husband was having an affair too. That certainly explained the lack of communication. I was so involved with my lover. We developed a very strong relationship. From Austria to the US we spoke on the phone twice a day and wrote daily. We planned to get married. He was divorced and I was hoping to get divorced. As the reality set in, I began to do a lot of thinking."

Kristen began to hesitate as her divorce drew near.

"I asked myself if it was love or gratitude I felt for this man. Had he saved me from a bad marriage or was he someone I was really in love with? He was eleven years older and attentive, supportive. We did a lot of talking and since I lacked that in the marriage, I knew he was the provider.

"At one point I wanted to have children with him and I most definitely thought of him constantly. That was the other side. I knew it all started when my husband couldn't make me happy. Sex was the least of it. It wasn't that great, to be honest. I guess I was more interested in his personality than in sex. My husband and I did not have a problem with sex–it was every other form of communication that failed. So I began to realize that this lover gave me what I needed. And then the distance, my being home and his being in Austria still, caused us to grow apart. We are in touch today but definitely not lovers. And probably we never will be again."

In looking back on this attachment, Kristen has "no guilt" and a "tremendous amount of gratitude."

"I was so unhappy in my marriage that I contemplated suicide. The affair was undeniably a way of fixing my husband, but it ended up really helping me. Had I not met my lover I would not have had this courage and strength to leave the marriage. Without this lover, I might still be there."

Once Kristen divorced her first husband, she became involved with a man who had been "only a friend" for years.

"We had never been romantically involved, and then one day he was with me and I had the thought that he belonged there, and one thing led to another. That was a very happy time for me, when we got married. But several months ago, he began to come home later and later. He's also in the military, and he is a recovered drug addict. He also comes from a family of only a father and brothers. His identification with women is limited, if existent at all. At first he came home late with excuses, then promises to stop, and finally I was so miserable that I ended up with a man at work. We had a brief affair because my husband was attached to someone.

"I needed him to be there to hug me and to tell me it was okay. I knew all along that this man wasn't what I wanted. But if sex was what it took, that was fine. I had to get by. The sex was all right, but nothing special. I had a decent sex life with my husband and I was very much in love with him. So when I went to this other man, it was not about sex. I let this one end fairly quickly."

Soon after, Kristen became involved with another man, a man she describes as "older and not a physical attraction."

"He is divorced and I'm getting divorced again. Although I do still love my second husband, I now know that he also carried on, and has impregnated another woman. That is why I need a lot of attention and talking to. This lover listens, which is the thing I like the most. He holds me and sex doesn't have to be included. He genuinely cares and knows when I'm in pain. We do things together, the movies, we go places. His attitude is that it's time I was treated right. The relationship is new and my feelings are mixed up so I'm not sure where it's going yet. In the past I was the giver. Next time around I want someone to give to me, someone to support me."

Kristen does not intend to conduct any other affairs.

"I feel these lovers most definitely helped me in a time of need. But I was raised not to have affairs. I would hope I'd never do it again. With my first marriage I had no guilt. With my second marriage I felt guilty despite how he treated me, because I do love him although he did something very wrong. I know now that affairs don't help to get back at anyone. My short affair was most likely a revenge affair; the rest was out of need and longing."

Marriage came into Kristen's life early on. She found it unsatisfying and disappointing. She opened herself up to other men in the hope that she could find more fulfillment. The outcome proved to be less than happy. Lacking sexual and emotional gratification, she continued in her search for a better connection with a man. What is notable is her persistence in finding these things for herself.

CஒலD

Nina

Nina is an extremely bright, well-educated woman who has been married for twenty years. After attending an excellent southern college, she found herself in love with a man whom her parents labeled "white trash." Her parents were "controlling" and discouraged the relationship. She unwillingly let the relationship go. Nina sees her break with this man as a turning point for her.

"That was the beginning of my mistake. I should never have given up a boyfriend I really loved and wanted to marry. My parents had different plans for me, and marrying a lawyer from a good family was their idea of perfect. They put so many obstacles in the way of the relationship that I did what they asked. I married this attorney and moved to Delaware. We bought a beautiful home; life seemed wonderful. We were relatively happy and several years later I had two children."

The marriage began to deteriorate when the elder child was seven.

"I began to notice that my husband came home later and later. Or he never went to bed at the same time I did. He'd go to bed later and get up earlier. Our sexual relationship began to cool. He stopped being interested in me sexually. I was very surprised. Any common bond seemed to be diverging. He began to collect art and he'd be out every weekend, seriously looking. He'd hang around the crowd that was into art or else he'd spend time with the people who were in the art business. I wasn't really drawn to it, although I tried.

"This lasted for a long time and finally I decided I wanted to go back to work, to join the work force. I found a job in a firm that was high-powered and social at once. I started to go to parties and luncheons that were business related. That was where I began to meet men. Several of them came to me, but I was afraid to respond . As sexually neglected as I felt at home, I was worried about hurting the marriage and I didn't want to do anything that would jeopardize my children."

At this point, Nina met her lover.

"There was one attractive man who was quite wealthy. I ran into him and we began to have an affair. We went to bed together that first time and since then it's been a steady thing. From the start he was good to me and I felt protected and loved.

"My lover and I have been together for several years. He is divorced and he'd like me to leave my husband for him. It is a serious relationship, almost as if we were the couple who is married. He showers me with gifts and treats me well; he pays attention to me. But my lover doesn't live in Delaware and I'm concerned about my children. I have this feeling that I'd have a difficult time getting the children if I got divorced and moved away. It's a real conflict for me, as much as I love this man. He would do anything for me. The relationship is everything that the marriage isn't. It's about sex, friendship, generosity and love. We share many interests and are very compatible. I'm torn between the life I want to have with him and my obligation to my children."

Nina's relationship with her husband has cooled on all levels by now and she realizes she is at a crossroads.

"I see this man as much as possible, several times a week. What began as an attachment, an attraction at a time in my life when I was very down and feeling rejected, has become a true love affair. I think that I hesitate to go forward with my lover because of the repercussions with my husband. I'm not only concerned about not getting to be with my children, but I'm worried that once I leave my husband he will come out of the closet. While I have no allegiance to my husband, I'm reluctant to have my children with him in that situation. I'm very worn out from thinking about my husband and what will happen if I go and how crazy I am about my lover. I want to move on with my life and my lover is waiting for me, but I hesitate because of my husband. I have not slept with my husband in years. I've slept only with my lover. If my lover is willing to keep things at the status quo, I'd be fine, I suppose. It's the push forward that changes everything."

Nina entered the marital relationship in an effort to please her parents. She seemed to feel trapped and neglected, emotionally and sexually. She then sought an affirming relationship with another man. On some level Nina is threatened by her husband and very concerned about the well-being of the children. She therefore continues the lover relationship but is crippled in her ability to move forward with it.

Cঙৎ০

Lucy

Lucy, the oldest of five children, characterizes her childhood as pleasant and her parents' marriage as intact. Once married, at the age of twenty, she moved to Texas, where she raised three children. Her marriage remained solid and happy for seventeen years. Today, at the age of forty-six, Lucy feels that her story is "not so unusual."

"As one approaches her late thirties, I believe there is curiosity on both sides–the wife's and the husband's. In my case, my husband became uninterested in the marriage. And we'd both married at such a young age that we knew very little sexually by our late thirties. Although I was very angry at my husband for pulling out of the marriage emotionally, I understood what was happening. I certainly didn't want my marriage to end, but I had a sort of European attitude toward it. I thought I should have an affair and remain married, and that if my spouse wanted to pursue an affair, he should remain in the marriage also."

Lucy met her lover on a tennis court two years after her father died, in a period when her marriage was in trouble.

"This was a time in my life when I was very open to men. My

'friend' was unmarried and available. I was able to see him once a week or more, at his apartment. The sex was excellent because he was so skilled. It was a learning experience for me. Although I was emotionally attached, I never considered leaving my husband for him. Yet he fulfilled a real need for me.

"I think that I was courageous enough to have the affair because my husband was emotionally and physically detaching from the marriage. At first I slept with both my husband and this man; eventually I had sex only with my lover. I know that some women sleep with their husbands more while they are conducting affairs, as if to keep the spouse off the track. But that wasn't the case with me."

Lucy's "friend" provided her with security and emotional support.

"Undeniably he was a father figure but we also had an important sexual relationship. Sex was a big part of the whole deal and I liked it a lot. I wasn't exactly obsessed, although I did think of this man all the time. I didn't feel guilty because my husband was so withdrawn. I realize now that my husband was one of those who behaved so badly in hope that he'd push me away and I'd leave him. I never wanted him to go, however. It wasn't how it worked."

Only after her first affair ended, a year and a half later, did Lucy realize that her husband had been having his own extramarital affair.

"My husband was so caught up in his own lies and deceit he never noticed how I was. I was too preoccupied with my life to catch on. In retrospect, I doubt I loved this man, but he made me feel good. Because I was approaching forty, it was an ego boost at a deflating time in my life. I'd been very down, a combination of my age and my married life. My 'friend' saw me throughout the ordeal. I felt so lucky to have him. He was there for me but never imposed on my space. I was lucky to have someone to sleep with when I decided to go outside the marriage. Maybe it was a back-burner affair, not real hot and sexy although we enjoyed each other sexually. I knew he'd had plenty of relationships, but it only made him more worldly and a better teacher."

The tryst ended because Lucy "became tired of it and the lack of emotion" which prevailed. It was at this juncture that she met another man, who was eleven years younger, and began a relationship with him.

"By then I wanted to get separated, from my husband because the marriage had truly dissolved. The man I met was such a contrast not only to my husband but to my previous lover, who had been over twenty years older than I was. This affair was wonderful. I loved being with someone who was so young. I got carried away with him and didn't notice how adolescent he really was. Instead I saw him as great fun and charming.

"I really was in love with him, but the age difference was a factor in terms of a serious relationship developing. It was a critical time in my life. There I was, making the decision to separate and subsequently divorce, and he was too callow to be emotionally supportive. Yet he was very sexy, almost too sexy for me to handle. It was hot. We did sex every possible way. He lived with someone, as did I, so it was a fling for both of us. For almost a year there was an intense, hot situation.

"The sex was wild and continual. I think a woman changes sexually between her twenties and late thirties and all that had been repressed, this young fling cut loose for me."

Lucy describes herself as encountering a tremendous amount of fantasy between her mid-thirties and forty.

"I finally began to wonder what was going on within my head, not only in the marriage, but what was out there, what I hadn't explored. From thirty-five to forty-five I've changed so much as a woman. I listen to women my age talk about sexuality and I get it. I became so much more interested in sex and in experimenting, in going beyond the experiences I knew. I'd had my children young, I watched them grow older–my life was in flux. I began to see marriage as a great trap. Although I'm over both affairs, they ended in friendship, so I've no regrets.

"Today I'm looking for someone my own age, having tried older and younger men. I don't want someone older in the long run, that I know. But I'm divorced now, and I feel youthful, as if I look better than ever before. I want someone who can keep up with me. What I like about being single is that I never know what's going to happen next. Not in the same way as when I was married–those interludes were calculated and planned. I feel really, truly free. I like that."

Lucy's interview is characteristic in certain ways. First of all, what she did was use the romance outside of her marriage as a means to separate herself from her husband. This resulted in an emotional and physical severing within the marriage. Eventually she was able to cut the marriage ties, because the affair had set her free.

The relationship also represented a sexual awakening and experimenting. Lucy was in it partly to make up for lost time, as if she were still an adolescent after so many years in a marriage, having had so little experience beforehand.

Lucy has gone through a process of being reborn. She is sorting out her identity as an adult woman.

CR8O

Sandy

Sandy is thirty-nine years old and lives in Miami. She has two children and is now almost divorced from her husband of six years. Her childhood was "very happy." She was overly protected while living at home and only when she arrived at college did she "discover her own sexuality." Sandy was surprised to find herself in the kind of marriage she had.

"It was a terrible marriage. He made me feel insecure, fat, stupid. There I was, taking care of the business and the kids while he had no job and still he made me feel like nothing. After three years of the marriage, I began to see someone. I had known my lover before I was married. He had asked me out when I was single but he was married, with several children, so I refused. At that point, I wasn't interested. But we were friends, and I'd see him at work. Then I was in a bad marriage and he asked me again and I accepted. I'm a strong believer in the right place at the right time. He said all the right things to me and the timing clicked. We began a serious relationship.

"He was fifteen years older and his children were grown. I was working and watching my small children so we were at different stages but it felt right emotionally. It was a wonderful sexual and emotional union and I never felt guilty. I was able to see him at least once a week. We rarely went out in public because my lover would get so nervous. Once or twice we were at a nice restaurant and he was so anxious, even on our anniversary. So mostly we used a friend's empty apartment."

Sandy had her affair because she was "disenchanted" with the marriage.

"My lover adored me. He thought I was beautiful and gave me everything I wanted. It was a very important relationship which did me a lot of good and gave me the confidence that I needed. The sex was loving and gentle but also uninhibited and open. While my husband and I fought constantly, my lover and I never fought."

Although Sandy did not leave the marriage because of her lover, she did feel the impulse to leave.

"I left for myself but he made me see why it was worth it to go. I was terribly unhappy by then. My lover offered to leave his wife for me but I didn't want him to break up his marriage. He had a great life, he was well-to-do and lived on a certain level. I understood I would only destroy him by encouraging him to leave all that. I was crazy about him but I knew him and he'd have gone nuts—of that much I'm convinced. I didn't want him to do it and he didn't believe me or forgive me. He thought I'd met someone else, someone new, but that wasn't it.

"It so happens that by then I had met my present lover. I was separating from my husband and I left my lover at the same time. I wanted to begin anew. I certainly didn't leave one for the other."

Sandy believes that her first lover had "plenty of affairs."

"I didn't care that he'd been around. He was the opposite of my husband, full of energy. He wanted to do things and I loved that. He was crazy in love with me. He would have left his wife for me. I know I would have married him but I couldn't do it. I'd have felt guilty if I'd broken it up, but I didn't feel anything wrong having been attached. We kept it a good secret.

"My husband never learned of this lover but he learned of the next one and he always suspected they were one and the same person. By the time I began to see my next lover I was living with my husband on again, off again. Both my ex-husband and my ex-lover were suspicious of my present lover. I tried to tell each of them that he was not the catalyst, but neither believed me.

Sandy describes her present lover as "exciting and sensual."

"He was very wealthy and great fun when we first met. I never knew where I'd end up when we went out, and I needed that. He was wild and crazy, the opposite of not only my husband but my older lover. And while the sex had been gentle and emotional with my first lover, this was a pure passion, very forceful sex. We did it eight times a night. It was not like anything I had ever known. It was beyond anything I had dreamed of.

"The relationship began on a sexual level and I knew I'd never been attracted to someone so physically, ever. Then it became more emotional. I was still living with my husband and I could only see this lover once or twice a week. He wouldn't leave his live-in until I'd left my marriage. I wasn't free to have a real relationship yet. I was just recovering from the loss of the first lover and telling myself it was the right thing to do. My first lover and I are still good friends. We continue to talk about it today. I know I'd never go back to him; it isn't possible."

Since Sandy left her first lover and became involved with the second, there have been "unexpected hardships."

"I went through an ugly divorce and he had some serious business problems. The real issues of life take away from the pure passion. But when it was a pure affair, for two years, it was the time of my life. I have never been sexually addicted to anyone else. What I had for a long while was a sexual obsession. He would do horrible things to me emotionally and it didn't matter. But eventually the relationship suffered because my husband was in the picture. Once he was finally gone, the affair turned into something more solid between this lover and myself. And then it was less exciting.

"As an affair-type thing, this was amazing. We'd have sex everywhere. We'd do it in restaurants, in the back of the movie theater. Wherever we were, we did it. If we went away we'd do it on a mountain cliff, on the beach, in the car all the time, in the buggy ride in New York City."

Only once her husband was out of the picture and Sandy's lover was no longer with his live-in did the romance settle into a "calmer situation."

"By then we were practically living together. It was very different. Having an affair is only fun but living together brings on the day-to-day stuff. It interferes with the excitement and a normal routine begins, about home and kids and work. The spontaneity was gone."

Although the "sexy" aspect of the relationship no longer predominated, Sandy tells us that she "never wanted to marry him."

"This is someone I've been with for three years. He was wild and nuts when we met and there's a part of him I still don't trust. Every year that goes by that we stay together, I wonder if we'll last. We were involved at first in a passionate, romantic way. What has gone on since then has changed it for sure. So many things interfered. We used to travel and go out all the time but now that my kids are older I can't leave them. So it keeps him home with me. My kids like him. He's been in my life for a long time.

"I suppose that after a terrible divorce and closing down a business I was a wreck. I am in no mood today to do anything in terms of the relationship. I don't want to marry him or anyone else at the moment. I want to be a mother, and feel financially stable."

However, Sandy believes that eventually she will move on–to the next relationship.

"Soon I'll be looking for someone new, but not yet. I'm not feeling like I can't live without this guy anymore, though. I realize we were the most intense when I was still married. But he loves me and my children and I think he'd like to stay. I'm with him until I meet someone who turns my head. I'm a passionate person but no one has spurred me on."

Sandy seems unhappy to still be with her lover but unable to detach. She was attracted to the second lover for the sex and to the first for affirmation. Ultimately neither lover worked out, which is why Sandy has to face the decision to move on. She needed the attention from these men during her marriage, yet fell into a bad way with each man. None of these men, not her lovers or her husband, have suited her needs.

CR80

Dana

Dana is from the Northeast and is fifty years old. She has been married for over twenty-five years and is "deeply in love" with her husband. She was drawn to the man who became her lover at work.

"There are major cultural differences between my husband and myself. The man I met at work shared the same interests I have. I love the arts, ballet and music. My husband watches every sport event possible on television."

Both she and her lover were married at the time and spent their time together mostly during the day.

"We'd meet for lunch. He wined me and dined me and was quite charming and suave. After a while he invited me to a show. That was how it began. My husband worked at night and I realized how simple it was to meet the other man. His wife was aloof and not involved with him and I doubt she cared what he did. The relationship centered around our common interest in culture. We really did not have terrific sex together, nor was it the main issue. We would speak for hours about music. I found him so intellectually stimulating, it was a delight."

The sex occurred as the relationship progressed.

"The sex was poor; in fact it was awful. He was older and not a great lover. Honestly, I was never satisfied, although I would never refuse him. I assumed it came with the package. We had sex in his apartment, and no one was ever there. But it was not spontaneous. None of our meetings were spontaneous and that was difficult. Everything had to be planned. I'd had affairs before so I understood how to play the game, that plans were necessary, but it began to tire me. I suppose I conducted this affair as a last hurrah. It was a true meeting of the minds, not for sex but for companionship and the attraction to the kind of man he was, the opposite of my husband. I have this insatiable ego and he was able to make me feel beautiful and smart, very clever and intellectual. I liked that. He was such an elegant man; there was a certain richness about him and he commanded respect. I think we came together because our spouses didn't appreciate a certain side in each of us. We found the appreciation in each other. While it was going on, for almost two years, it was a dalliance–delightful, forbidden fruit."

Her feeling toward her husband remained the same throughout the duration of the affair.

"I adored my husband the entire time. I was in control from the beginning and my marriage was never in jeopardy. I needed this relationship for myself; it was only for me. I wanted other things from this lover than from my husband–that was clear to me from day one. I wasn't worried about my husband finding out because I always knew how he felt about me. I held on to the hope that if he did discover anything, he would understand. Despite the fun of the intellectual pursuit it offered, if I had had to make a choice I would have said no to my lover."

The relationship Dana shared with her lover did not end abruptly, but "dwindled, withered and died."

"It was never going to go anywhere. It was a no-win situation. That is the nature of these things and one knows that from the start. And as I mentioned, I've had other affairs, so I was prepared. I am continually drawn to men. And men are drawn to me. He was one of them. I believe that if women have an opportunity to partake in this kind of adventure, it adds something to their life. It makes you feel young and beautiful to have men desire you, at any age. I knew the stakes, the risks and the rewards from the outset. Yet my age made me feel this affair was important. I knew the opportunities were lessening. I engaged myself in every part of it for as long as possible.

"I still perceived myself as a sexual being, no matter what my age. I've had other affairs and when I think of them, I feel that this one was meaningful because it happened when it did. It was something I no longer expected and there it was, something only for me, something I have just for myself. There was no cruel ending or pain, just an end. And while it lasted it was great. We were both mature and adult enough to go forward. I never felt an ounce of guilt, nor have I ever, in an extramarital affair."

Dana embarked on a lover relationship as if it were a project. She wanted to know if she was still desirable and sexy. A man outside the marriage was able to do that for her. Dana's love affair was a temporary expedient, and she was capable of taking from it what she needed and moving on.

ᘓᔆᕲ

Abigail

Abigail is from a small town in the Northeast, where she presently lives. She is in her mid-forties and was married at eighteen. Coming from a stable family background, Abigail married happily, and had children, before she began to question her marriage.

"I was not very bright to marry so early, but it started off swell. After twelve or thirteen years it became arid and stale. I think it was a combination of my husband busting his chops. He was short-tempered and overworked. We had problems with the kids and I worked full-time. We were stressed and stretched and neither found time for the other."

At this time Abigail met the man who would become her lover.

"I'd gone to a business luncheon and this guy was really nice. He had something to offer me businesswise. I hadn't been looking for an affair–it never even occurred to me. He was married too, and close to my age. He also had kids but they were away at school. He lived in another state, so we would make plans to meet each other. It began with lunch and for a period of six months I'd meet him as often as I could, depending on our schedules. Once or twice a week– I was a slow starter. It took five or six times to get together to have sex.

"We'd go to his home. I wouldn't go to a local hotel or to my house. I'd park at a shopping center and we'd get into his car together. The first time that we went to his house I was so stupid I didn't even know what would happen. I only knew his wife was not in town."

Abigail describes the sex as "pretty good but not great."

"Soon after I began to have sex with my lover I stopped having sex as often with my husband. I vacillated between feeling like a piece of shit, to feeling like I deserved this, I needed it. It was difficult for me to handle two men. There was such guilt, which I blame on my upbringing.

"I thought my partner was hot stuff. I was very attracted to him and he made me feel good at a time when it was greatly appreciated. It was a boost which my ego sorely needed. My God, I really cared about how I looked and how I appeared. The relationship was definitely eighty-five percent physical. I wasn't in love with him but I thought of him all the time. We'd talk on the phone. Basically I'd call his private number and we'd talk for long periods.

"The relationship taught me a lot of things. I'm grateful for that. We were from very different backgrounds. I always wanted a tall, blond, blue-eyed guy. And when you're married at eighteen, where could you have been? I'd been nowhere. This was quite an awakening for me. He taught me things in bed, too. Then the relationship developed into an emotional attachment. I wondered about that— was it because he'd put me on a pedestal compared to my home life, that I responded as I did?"

Despite her suspicion that her partner had had many lovers, Abigail believes that he would have left his marriage for her.

"For me it was an isolated incident, but he seemed so experienced, so cool about it. I told no one about it, which means I got to a point where my nerve endings were gone, shot. My lover began to press me to take a stand and it was then that I decided to give my marriage another chance. First of all, I was afraid. And secondly, I felt I owed it to my husband, who never knew of the extramarital relationship, to make a go of it. I needed to share my life with him. That was what it was all about. So we had this showdown and I told my husband how I felt. Deep down I was in love with my husband, not my lover, but I was repulsed by the marriage on some level. Not only my husband, but my family. I understand it wasn't a good period in my life."

Abigail realized that the prolonged relationship with her partner was what forced her to reevaluate her marriage.

"I couldn't lead a double life anymore. Knowing what it entails, I couldn't begin to do it again. My lover saw that I was mildly crazed. He understood that I was confronting my husband. He was hoping my husband would refuse my request for more, for a better marriage. But that wasn't how it ended. Instead my husband agreed and made a concerted effort, and I left the affair. The affair had become a deep emotional attachment, something that retaught me how to care and be romantic. I really enjoyed giving and taking. It was a wonderful insight into a life I'll never touch again.

"I never got over the guilt as far as my children were concerned. I still feel guilty and sometimes I feel like blurting something out, like telling my husband the whole story. I doubt he had an affair but if he did, then he certainly wouldn't have been in it for the emotional attachment. I guess the bottom line is that I don't want to know about it."

Several months ago Abigail unexpectedly ran into her lover.

"I thought my heart would drop. We didn't know many people in common and it was such a surprise. Then I thought of him afterwards. In a blue moment I find myself thinking of him. I know women who have lovers for all sorts of reasons. I have one friend with a much older husband. Because her marriage is lacking, she goes to the airport to find businessmen when flights are canceled or delayed in bad weather. I could never do this–besides the emotional emptiness, I'm afraid of contracting a disease. Those are purely physical encounters, and I was never in it for that alone."

Abigail used her lover to improve her feelings about herself. Then she realized she preferred the marriage. This realization came about as a process, a kind of self-awareness after the attention she received from the lover. She really took the relationship and used it to revise the marriage. This worked well for her.

CRED

Hanna

Hanna is forty-two and lives in northern California, having grown up in Los Angeles. She has been married for twenty years, in a marriage she tells us is "dysfunctional." Her parents were divorced when she was eighteen, a breakup Hanna describes as "something that happened too late." For her the damage had already been done and she chose marriage to prove she could make a go of it.

"I unquestionably married my husband to prove my father was wrong about him. I doubt I was even in love, but there was something special between us. My husband and I were the same age, very young, when we met at nineteen, and my father, a jealous father, wouldn't acknowledge our relationship. To him, no one was good enough for me. He saw a pattern in Tom, my husband's, family. Because Tom's father had left his wife, he believed that Tom would make a wretched husband and leave me. But my father trusted no one; he was very suspicious.

"I consider my marriage to be one of subtle abuse. Finally, having my spirit broken many times, so that I felt I was worthless and could do nothing, I was driven elsewhere. I had no skills to do it any other way. I think that therapy helps, but one has to have enough money to afford therapy and by then so much has gone on, so much is in disrepair."

Hanna has two children and has worked throughout the course of her marriage to Tom.

"I'm not a person who likes to stay at home. I've always worked at least part-time, as a teacher. I've taught high school, university and college levels. During this career, I've met many men. But I thought it was dangerous to have male friends because my marriage was unhappy. I thought I'd be tempted to get involved. Only recently have I cultivated male friends. Not everyone has to be romantic or sexual. Now I know.

"Through these men I've befriended, I've learned that I'm still very attractive and have a lot to offer. I like myself today. If I choose to be alone, that's different than being forced to be alone in a bad marriage. I assumed I was inadequate all the time. My husband allowed me to become dependent, although to the outside world no one saw me that way, which amazed me. I saw my dependency as an act to get back Tom for not including me in his life."

The other men who entered Hanna's life made her feel "worthy."

"About a year ago I began a rebound relationship with someone I'd known for over ten years. He is a few years older than I am and divorced. I knew him because he worked for my husband in some capacity. I'd always been aware that he was attracted to me. I knew in pursuing this relationship that I would not be rejected, and that was important. I needed to be wanted, and he thought I was wonderful. I also wanted to have sex with John.

"The sex was very exciting in the beginning. We made a real effort to make it work and make it good. I think we were willing to put the effort into it because we knew what the result would be. I'd see him daily sometimes, other times a few days a week, so there was lots of sex. My children never liked John and I don't know if I love him, but the relationship has been a very positive thing for me from the start."

Hanna chose to be with John when Tom, her husband, informed her that "all women had become interesting to him, even unattractive ones."

"At first I told Tom that I would be content to be alone with him. He was already in a relationship with a married woman. That knowledge colored my opinion. I no longer wanted to be amicable or to consider his request for a trial separation. I didn't like this woman replacing me in any way, although I was involved with John. I did not like feeling deceived, no matter what I was doing or why I was doing it. My husband never said he loved me or that he was committed to our relationship, and my revenge relationship became more intense as I considered this.

"John is so different from Tom. I'd been with Tom for so many years it was quite an experience. I think of my relationship with John as a Cinderella/prince attraction. I always knew it might happen with this guy. I also knew it would never be long-term, which would make it safe. If temporary, I thought, then it's not an emotional investment. If I fell for someone, it would be trouble. So I purposely chose John, who has always rushed over to me at parties and was definitely interested. I felt accepted by him, and that was the most important part."

Because Hanna perceived her lover's acceptance, she was able to play out their sexual fantasies.

"The lovemaking was more feminine; he was a more feminine lover. And we'd set the stage, set the scene. It was romantic, with candles and music. He courted me and it was very passionate and lots of fun. The fantasies were things I would have done with my husband if he'd been willing. But with John there was no question that he was willing.

"I was emotionally starved too, and I found it exciting to take walks together in the field, to have lunch together. Having lunch with someone is really romantic. What was especially exciting to him was when I played with his genitals while he was driving. It was pretty interesting that he liked it. I tried things out with him that I imagined my husband would want. I began to recognize that passion can be re-created in a long-term relationship if one plans ahead and works harder on the sex. After a certain time with a lover, it's the same. The passionate part keeps demanding work and energy.

"We'd stay at guest houses together. He had no money for fancy hotels and I didn't want to get involved with that part. I realized that I'd been seen as a wife for so long that something as simple as going where my lover wanted to go, and feeling close when we did, was enough."

Hanna believes that she and her husband had begun an open marriage at this stage.

"Our situation was on again, off again. We spoke of separation but we were together too. My husband only wanted to know if I was having sex with John. He tried to get emotionally involved with my life while he struggled with his own. He had a lover then and when she left him he actually sought out my comfort. My relationship with John made me see myself as a whole person and I rejected my husband's needs. John was reinforcing, telling me that our mutual friends liked me. He made me feel beautiful. He'd tell me what Tom would never say, and we encouraged each other. I think that it is one of those situations where we both had needs and the needs were met. I knew we could fill those needs, so when it was done, it changed the character of the relationship. I feel now that we are more friends than anything."

Hanna "never felt guilty" during her tryst with her lover, although she was concerned about AIDS.

"I was careful and used condoms because my children and husband were at risk. I worried a lot about AIDS with my husband and I nagged him to use condoms because I knew he was having sex. In a strange way I was happy for Tom to explore other women because I felt he'd come back to me that way. My impression, having been exposed to men in their late thirties and forties, is that it's no longer the one-night-stand performance of one's twenties. Men themselves—their bodies, the bodies of older men—do not want one-night stands; they want the real thing, a mature woman, for a performance. It's interesting, how this pushes me back toward my marriage.

"Today I only want to have a traditional marriage and no more relationships outside the marriage. I see now that both my husband and I should work harder on our partnership. I learned I can only handle sex with one person at a time because to me it means a real commitment. I still believe that the romance with John changed me, for the better, and that my husband can change for the better. The attachment to my marriage is what I'm after. Yet I'm determined to not lose my new identity. I've regained that identity by going outside my marriage with Tom, in order to return to it. Other men have made me realize I'm likable, dynamic, very attractive, and it works. I think of my father and my mother. I see that I became like my father, a passive, nonconfrontational spouse, in order to avoid becoming like my mother, who baited my father constantly. Not only my attachment to John, a lover, but my reevaluating the marriage on its own terms has made me know that I do not have to repeat anyone's mistakes. I can succeed."

The primary motivation for Hanna to marry was to heal the dysfunctional family she hoped to leave behind. Thus she became involved with her first lover when the marriage did not compensate for her past. Hanna has sought affirmation in other men, and now hopes to return to the marriage a stronger person. It is as if Hanna were more attached to the marriage than to her husband per se. Her desire to maintain the marriage outweighed whatever sexual affirmation she received from her lovers. Here we see a tremendous need to repair and remain in the primary structure that she built with her spouse.

ఴ౬ఴ

Rebecca

Rebecca is twenty-nine years old and comes from a close-knit working-class family in northeastern Pennsylvania. Her parents divorced, remarried each other, and divorced again. Today they live together but are not married. Her upbringing was "strong and ethnic" despite the "hot-and-cold" relationship her parents shared. Rebecca was married at the age of twenty-five and is divorced.

"My marriage was to a man fourteen years older. I was crazy about him and I thought that he was a lot more sexual than he really was. From the start, we did not have sex as much as I expected. He was not a very up person and I'm a very up person. At first I believed that I could bring him up but eventually I lost the desire to do it anymore. After a while, he no longer responded to me. I couldn't make him feel happy."

At this time, Rebecca was working full-time and "did not think about other men."

"But there was someone who was after me. He'd been after me since I was single and he was married. I'm in the retail business and this man was always coming by the shop. He was a customer. He'd purchase things as an excuse to come into the store. He was fifteen years older than me and had a child close to my own age. I wasn't attracted at first because I was so preoccupied with my boyfriend, who became my husband. This man would proposition me. He'd say, let's go to lunch or dinner, and I'd say no. This went on for two years. Then I got married and he was divorced and remarried for some time. Then my marriage began to stop working and this man was there. Finally, my husband lost his job and by then I was sad and sick of it.

"This man, who is very powerful, knew that my husband was looking to be interviewed for a new job and so he set him up. He arranged for him to have an interview and he got him the plane ticket and all along I knew what he was doing. I knew that he arranged it so he could be with me. I couldn't believe that he went to that amount of trouble to be with me. My husband went off on his interview and we went to dinner. We were definitely supposed to sleep together. He made no bones about it, about wanting to sleep with me that night. But I didn't do it the first time. He was fine about it; he said there would be other times. He said he didn't want to do it with me only once so he didn't push, he waited. But we were at a Marriott hotel and I was afraid."

Rebecca describes her lover as "very clever and patient." The second time that they were together, his "scheme" worked.

"I slept with him. It was strange to sleep with two people at the same time. But I wasn't having much sex with my husband. It wasn't as if it was sex with my lover all afternoon, sex with my husband all night. I suppose after this relationship with the other man had gone on for some time, my husband noticed I wasn't asking for sex anymore, but he wasn't really macho. He only talked a good story. In other words, my husband didn't demand the sex. I had been the instigator from the start."

Since their initial encounter, Rebecca and her lover have been together at least two times a week for the past three years.

"I really am in love with him. I know he'll never leave his wife. But we were friends first and I turned him down between wives, so I don't demand anything now. And because we are such good friends, I can't imagine it ever ending. But there's the sex, too. I don't mind sharing him with his wife. I admit I'd like to have him to myself, but there's no choice.

"We get along very well. He's a very wealthy man and I sometimes think that it is because of his work and career that he thinks he ought to be married—it looks good. He needs to fill a certain public picture. I have seen him with his wife and I don't understand how it works. She might suspect something but I don't believe she wants to ask. And he takes the chance of getting caught. We all live in the same town. Only my close friends and his close friends know about us."

In the past six months, Rebecca has become divorced.

"Now that I'm divorced, my lover is my protector. He takes care of me big time. He treats me like a queen. Emotionally he's the best. So I still accept the situation. I'm happy the way it is. My lover did worry when I first decided to get divorced that I'd want him to leave his marriage, that I'd make demands. But that was not my plan. I knew he wasn't available, and my getting divorced was for me, not for my lover.

"I remember how this affair started. In the beginning, when we were both available, the attention was all on his side. I thought of it as an affair of the mind. I always avoided him at the very start. During my marriage I had cancer and my husband was great but my lover helped me find the right doctors and he helped me through a difficult time. My husband knew he was helping, but he never knew he was my lover. To this day, now that I am fine, my husband doesn't know what went on."

Rebecca describes the sex with her lover as "very different" than with her husband.

"He's more attentive. My lover gets excited talking about it and my husband wouldn't ever discuss it. I tried to seduce my husband all the time. I would put on negligees and always I had to start the sex. Never have I had to initiate sex with my lover. He did come on to me at first and now it's comfortable, a shared sexual desire. It's a nice feeling to be appreciated sexually and mentally. If I began to talk with my husband he wouldn't even put down the magazine he was reading. No matter how important or trivial the matter, he ignored me. My lover listens to anything I have to say.

"He is the opposite of my husband in every way. Now I think of my lover as very handsome but in the beginning my husband seemed handsomer. It depends on how you look at someone."

Rebecca hopes to continue in this relationship for as long as it succeeds.

"We never talk about the future in terms of my remarrying or his divorcing. Yet I'm very happy. I have no regrets about having begun the affair. If I ever marry again, I can't say I won't stop seeing him. If I had the choice I'd never ever stop seeing him. I have no intention of stopping the affair."

The affirmation offered by Rebecca's lover was so compelling that she couldn't resist. Her attachment to this man was understandably all-encompassing. She almost relishes the setup and only hopes it will continue.

sex-driven

affairs

2

Sex-Driven Affairs

INTRODUCTION by DR. DONALD COHEN

Dr. Donald Cohen has a master's degree in social work and a Ph.D. in clinical psychology. He is a certified marriage and family therapist. In Connecticut. Dr. Cohen hosts his own television/radio show, "Kids Are Talking."

When first approached, Dr. Cohen explained that there are no absolutes in a marriage or in the reality of an extramarital affair.

"One cannot be too simplistic in looking at the dynamic of the situation, and while there are similarities in many of these relationships, each tale has unique qualities. Often money is the motivating force that holds a marriage together. Another 'glue' is the fear of breaking up a family, taking away the stability that the children rely on. The third concern has to do with custody battles and the long, drawn-out agony of divorce.

"Despite these issues, I have seen a significant increase in extramarital affairs in the last five years, particularly with women in their late thirties and early forties. I think it is a time in their lives when they are beginning to experience physical change, and the need and desire to remain youthful become important. Many of these relationships are about self-esteem. As children grow up and are over the hump, the basic problem of a midlife crisis sets in. A certain restlenessness sets in, and the question gets asked, have their needs been met in the marriage?

"These women want to bust out and have fun. If there has been no career and no way to reenter the work force, there is no place for them to put this energy.

"There is a feeling that monogamy is obsolete and that it is possible to connect to another person on many different levels. Women who have security in a marriage do not always have the passion, the soulful, intellectual connection. Some women express a desire to have that plus the passion all in one person. But the question is, could they have passion when sharing a bathroom on a daily basis?

"Women are looking for enjoyment and freedom. Occasionally they become bored and seek a more free-spirited relationship, a less attached situation. What is appealing about the other man is the lack of attachment. That very lack of attachment becomes a form of passion.

"There is a tremendous amount of projection tied into these affairs. If a woman finds something lacking in her life or within herself, she is more apt to focus on someone else. These are the women who marry a man to fill in the undeveloped part of themselves and then they gradually develop that missing part. Eventually the need for the married partner no longer exists. So this woman gets her act together, the projected other side that was missing is now integrated, and she has outgrown her spouse.

"The possibility of a woman genuinely falling for another man often arises. Some of these relationships are absolutely more than a physical attraction. Sometimes they are truly love affairs. And the idea of being in love with two people at the same time is valid. To expect any one person to meet all of another person's needs is unrealistic. So while affirmation in terms of one's attractiveness and self-esteem is at the core of the situation, it does not negate what someone might feel for someone else. We cannot rule out the prospect of loving more than one person. That brings us to the 'mental affair,' which is in a class by itself."

In exploring the mental affair, Dr. Cohen notes that unconsummated attachments are very common.

"The 'mental affair' is not physical, but a condition of being drawn in by someone's mind in an intellectual/emotional way. Often in a mental affair the lover resists the woman who is interested because he doesn't wish to cause any pain for her and her family or for himself and his family. A single man who enters into an affair with an older woman might resist because he doesn't want to be attached; nor does he want her to be attached. He hopes to avoid complications by avoiding the affair. Then the mental affair is in play. The 'fatal attraction' aspect of an affair is less likely with a mental affair. So while there can be physical attraction it is not acted upon, for a variety of reasons."

The older woman/younger man scenario is actually quite common in a physical relationship.

"For women hitting their late thirties to early forties, this is frequently an appeal to feel young and attractive. In this case, there is less of an emotional attachment that drives the relationship. What we underestimate is how many women view their husbands as boring sexually and how this sensation can bring about a physical attachment to someone else.

"It is this kind of attachment that causes such upset when a husband discovers an affair. I am struck by how jealous they are about the sexual acting out, and how less threatened they are by any emotional connection. For many women, if the emotional connection is the hook, their husbands don't seem to get that. In certain cases, I believe that counseling can wake up the spouse to be more attentive to his wife's desires—whether to be a better lover or a better emotional supporter. A husband can learn techniques, if he is willing and open-minded. Marriage requires constant energy, in terms of sex and emotions. Be it a new position, a new way of touching and technique, or an effort to be honest and open in the marriage, the couple requires constant, mutual attention. If these needs cannot be met in the marriage, women will look elsewhere. I see many times that a woman will react by choosing a lover who is the opposite of her husband, because she cannot be wrapped up in one person and her need to break free constitutes a newness, a freshness in the form of a lover."

Dr. Cohen strongly believes that marital therapy is beneficial in certain instances.

"If a couple gets into counseling, and the couple is willing to explore the roots of the affair, there can be less damage. Mostly an affair by either spouse is not the cause of marital problems but symptomatic of a problem within the marriage. There can be a situation where a woman learns how to be a better lover and brings that back to the marriage, actually enhancing the marriage. Or while in counseling it might come out that a woman feels her husband has abandoned her and the affair is a manifestation of a woman crying in the dark, attempting to get her husband's attention. Or there is a sense of feeling rejected in the marriage and needing to go outside the marriage for that attention."

According to Dr. Cohen, specific circumstances trigger the choice for a woman to find another partner.

"The first of these involves women who associate their husband with their family, the family of origin, a father or brother, and cannot have a romantic attachment to that man. It is a relationship like brother–sister, and not a positive one for a marriage. If this woman has never separated from her family, it is as if she never left home. The woman who has never had a healthy break from her family ends up recapitulating what hasn't been resolved in her family of origin with her husband. This is not too sexy a setup.

"Another category is incest. Women who have experienced incest as young girls or women will be prone to have affairs. Because the husband is once again associated with the family of origin, the desire to break free, to have an affair with someone outside that 'family,' is very strong. These women are in search of a man who is not part of the system. These lovers are perceived as offering a whole new life. The lover is the ticket to emotional autonomy.

"However, these women are often drawn to a more physical relationship. It can be a very intense attachment as a result of their difficulty. What is too threatening for them is the association with the original incestuous trauma.

"A third category is a woman who comes from a dysfunctional family. This woman tends to repeat the same types of destructive patterns in her own marriage. There is a restlessness in her marriage and with her own family as she realizes she is repeating what her mother and father did. This is a trend that can also be improved with therapy and self-awareness."

Dr. Cohen concludes with a prediction of increased romances outside marriage in the future.

"Ultimately, I see extramarital affairs on the rise. Women become more and more sophisticated, owing to the women's movement and a stronger sense of entitlement, a raised and liberated consciousness; it is inevitable. The desire to explore is so strong, and while discovery is a risk, if women want to do it, they will do it. The threat of discovery reflects how much risk one is willing to take for the sake of the 'reward.'

"Society is so stressful and complex, moving at such a rapid pace; people are more and more rootless. At a time when the traditional American family is being threatened, modern women cannot help but acknowledge their internal and external needs in the form of a lover."

CRESO

Priscilla

Priscilla, in her early forties, comes from a small town in Pennsylvania, where she experienced a typical middle-class upbringing. After some college, she left to be married. She had a son soon after and was widowed when he was quite young. She then married a man whom she knew from childhood. Unexpectedly, he began a job in another city, spending Monday through Friday there. Despite what Priscilla describes as "appreciating Henry," she did begin a relationship with someone else at this time. Although Priscilla assured us that money was never a motivation, the connection to a man as provider/protector seems significant.

"I owe Henry a great deal. He was very supportive when my husband died, toward me and toward my child. But then he began to travel and I became lonely. I was at a museum opening and I met a man. He was the same age as I, and he had just been divorced. He was well known in his field, which was a departure for me. What he did for a living was also unique in my experience."

Priscilla was "attracted to this man immediately" and after meeting innocently for coffee a few times, they began a love affair without the knowledge of her mate.

"Henry never knew, not that he paid any attention to me at this stage. After the energy he gave me when I was widowed, he had become preoccupied with his business and neglected me. I realized I needed attention and I sought it outside the marriage. As soon as my husband left on Monday morning for his job and the kid went to school, my lover came over and we spent the entire day together. It was wonderful, absolutely fabulous. During the winter we'd spend the whole day in bed, leaving only to prepare lunch or to retrieve the mail. The sex was nonstop and quite different from anything I'd ever expected. I became so attached to him. It was not like any relationship I'd ever known. He always left at three o'clock, just before my child returned from school. That was our pattern.

"We filled each other's needs, emotionally and physically. He was very attentive and heard what I had to say but he also knew what I liked in bed. We were very careful not to be seen together in our small town. During the warmer months we'd go out only to places where we knew no one would recognize us. We did a lot of picnicking. This relationship we shared, almost like a minimarriage, was more intense and satisfying than anything I'd ever known."

They worked their schedules carefully and saw each other on a daily basis.

"In the summer when my child was home, we met at his house. And sometimes if there was an art opening or event at night during the week, I'd meet him there, cautiously. But we never, in two years, saw each other on weekends. I never even telephoned him on weekends, when my husband was at home. My lover accepted this setup and never pressured me, although he was divorced and free. I never wanted to hurt my spouse in any way—that wasn't the intent of the affair. I felt guilty; he'd been so supportive and kind, as I said. I always reasoned that it was for me, my tryst with my lover, that it had little to do with anyone else."

Priscilla tells us that had her husband not taken a job in another town she would never have conducted an affair.

"The attachment to my spouse was too great. When he was there, physically and paying some attention to me, it was enough. I was fulfilled. But when he became immersed in business and did not seem himself, I really felt rejected and unhappy. I'm fortunate to have found someone so special to suit my needs at the time."

During this interval, Priscilla and her lover saw each other every weekday.

"And our love for each other never changed or waned. We were as connected to each other after two years as we'd been from the start. The sex was terrific and we were so devoted. It was as if he provided my weekday sexual/emotional connection and Henry became the weekend lover. As if I had two lovers or two spouses."

The affair ended when Priscilla's husband obtained a job nearer to their home and no longer traveled. She felt she could not take the risk of exposure.

"I think I made it clear to my lover from the start that ultimately I'd choose my husband. He accepted that. Still, I was very sorry to see the day come. And it was difficult to let go."

Her marriage eventually grew more solid as she pulled away emotionally from her lover.

"I felt very sad when the love affair ended. The relationship had been such a constant factor in my life, it was a withdrawal, a physical wrenching. But the end coincided with Henry's return, and in retrospect it was inevitable. Not that I had a problem with the setup, but when the pattern was about to shift, I knew I wasn't able to sustain both."

With her husband home more, the initial closeness returned. After a time, they had a baby together. Priscilla expressed satisfaction with the situation.

"I am relieved that Henry and I are reunited and that we have a child, another boy. I could not have married my lover; it wasn't a consideration. Yet there's not a day that goes by that I don't think of him and the 'hideaway' relationship that we shared."

Priscilla romanticized her relationship with her lover and then landed on her feet again with the reality of marriage. Because she is a conventional type, there was little question that she would return to the marriage. The entire episode was limited in scope, and restricted to a finite period.

As often is the case, Priscilla conducted her affair as if it existed in its own sphere. She was able to 'split.' She separated her actions and emotions from the rest of her life. What is distinctive about her situation, however, is that while her activities with her lover were circumscribed, her thoughts and connections were obsessive.

Despite being married twice, Priscilla is clearly traditional in terms of her orientation. While she stumbled on to a relationship with a lover, it was not necessarily the result of a marital situation. Yet it seems that her sexual intimacy with the other man highlighted problems within the marriage. The second phase of the lover situation was her obsession with the sexual aspect of the romance. The sexual attachment to this partner was all-enveloping.

౷౸

Cynthia

Cynthia, who is in her late forties, has had three husbands and "many" affairs. Growing up in the suburbs, she was married for the first time at the age of twenty. The marriage lasted two years and there were no children. Because of her sheltered childhood Cynthia's awareness of other men did not begin until the end of this marriage. Since then she has been continually drawn to men, as if making up for lost time.

"I was in love with my first husband. He was two years older and from a wealthy family but my parents were not pleased. They thought we were too young and that he was not of the same social caliber.

"Then I began to change. I was twenty-two, and unhappy. We had a dear friend who was several years older and he seemed to have a jet-set life; he was always out. I didn't see my life that way. I was too young to feel that I'd missed out."

She married again a year after her divorce and describes her second husband as very different from the first.

"He was foreign and very strong. He was self-confident. And because he was from another country, there were no in-laws to deal with. They lived there, not here, and there were no problems. But he had no money and worked hard, unlike my first husband, who was wealthy. We had one child and were married for seven years.

"At first I only had eyes for him, until we had money problems and a kid. Then it got complicated—you know, in a city a one-bedroom apartment is what everyone has before children. Everyone is on equal footing. Your needs are simple. It got complicated with a child. It had been easier before. At that time I began to feel like I was hanging around. Being a housewife was not great. I'd always worked. I began to feel trapped.

"Also, I'd just quit smoking and gained weight. Then I lost it. At this party I met a man. He approached me and made a fuss. That was when I had my first affair, with that guy. He was married also. The affair lasted a year. It was a once-a-week thing. If we had spent more time together than that, in bed, it might have lasted longer. Outside the marriage, a great deal of sex is what counts. It has to be very sensual.

"My husband never found out about it, about that particular affair. And while it was going on, I felt the same about my husband as I'd felt before the affair began. He didn't enter into it. Six days a week I was a wife and mother. And once a week I was a lover and had a lover. I'd begun to work again, and I was taking classes. But it was the affair that made me feel terrific. He made me feel special, desirable, sexy. In retrospect, it was probably not a good thing that it began because it made it so much easier the next time. You know, sort of like killing someone. The next time it's easier—although I'm not much on guilt. I felt entitled."

When asked how she might have felt had she known her husband was having an affair, she told us that she wouldn't care.

"I believe he should do what he wants and not tell me, no confessions, and I'll do the same. After all, when people lived until thirty and married at fifteen, the men were off on the crusades and the women were busy at home, so it worked. It was so different then and life was hard. Everyone had responsibilities. I think it's as we become a leisure society that these affairs begin."

Cynthia's first affair ended because of the "emotional attachment."

"Later, my other affairs worked better, when I wasn't so attached. They were about sex and that proves the most successful affair—when it's only about sex. If women fall in love with their lovers, it's not easy. As I began to find myself in the workplace I had a convenient excuse to go out, on business, and I met men. The men varied in type and occupation and eventually the first liaison ended. I was free then to arrange dates. Everything lightened up. I loved the freedom."

Although Cynthia did not consider leaving her husband for the first lover, she admits that she had wanted to be more important to him than she believes she was. In her next encounter she became involved with someone she worked with, a man she'd known for a long while.

"He was crazy about me, and he probably got divorced for me, but I did not get divorced for him. I did get divorced, but not for him. It was an affair that lasted many years. At times I think I might have been in love with him. But then I understood myself. He wasn't successful enough for me. I'd been married to a man [second husband] who at the start I thought was quite wonderful, but his business reversals caused trouble. I knew I needed a certain lifestyle to be comfortable and this man couldn't provide it. The main attraction was sexual. He was a terrific lover and we had a great sex life all the time. But he was very nurturing when I needed to feel important. I suppose we were very attached and our lives were intertwined. There I was again with something more than just the physical, no matter how hard I tried."

Yet this lover was not the man who became Cynthia's third husband. The man she is presently married to was someone she met on a blind date. Describing her present husband, Cynthia tells us that he is a "very good provider."

"He's very bright, funny, and adores me. Still, I don't rule out having affairs. As I get older, men seem less attractive, but I've always wanted to be with men. I have had many affairs and I plan to keep having them.

"There is nothing like a new relationship, whether one is newly married, divorced and dating, or having an affair. It's the best high in the whole world. If people could sustain this euphoria, there'd be no need to have liquor, drugs. But eventually it settles down to a routine. And once it gets to a routine, it's much less exciting. There needs to be a meeting of the minds. Sex is no longer enough. I once had an affair with a high-powered, smart man. He was a good lover but it was also the conversation before and after the sex that was fascinating. These lovers take you outside the ordinary, daily routine. You see, I believe in affairs because they add something to your life—not necessarily to your marriage, but to your life."

In terms of the risk to a marriage, Cynthia concedes that men do not like sharing their wives.

"Men are children. If you ever notice boys playing together, they say, 'It's *my bat*, my ball, my turn.' Girls share but boys cannot. I don't believe we're really of the same species. Men are not particularly nice, and for the most part they don't particularly like women. So the answer is that it *is* a risk to a marriage.

"In my second marriage I went away with my lover to a nice place. We had a great weekend, and then I got caught. Freud might say I wanted to get caught, but when confronted, I hadn't one iota of guilt or remorse. I explained to my husband that I wasn't getting what I needed from the marriage, that things weren't going well. Sure, there was the risk that he'd leave, but he didn't. I think he was hurt and upset and unhappy, although I didn't really care. I apologized for his finding out more than for the actual act. While I don't voluntarily want to hurt anyone, I was happy I'd had that weekend with my lover. Besides, people often know when a spouse is cheating. Certain patterns develop. That's how one gets caught."

Cynthia views herself as a person who has more rapport with men than most women.

"Since I was married three times, and attractive, women were never keen on keeping me as a friend. Still, I think that women are smarter than men as a rule, and in general more clever. I see women as continually left out, even in the top echelons of business. None of that has changed. I think they have affairs to get back at men, to say this is something you can't control. I can do it, so can you, but you can't take it away from me. I can do it just as well and just as often. Realizing this, and being experienced, I no longer fall in love with my lovers. I no longer need to justify an affair. And I believe many women are coming to the same conclusion, that they do it to stroke their own ego or to wreak havoc and revenge on the men they live with.

"The double standard is just as strong today as ever. It is a feather in a man's cap to have an affair. He's real macho and a woman is seen as a sleaze. To me, men are pigs, they're all chauvinists, even the best of them. It sounds trite and old hat, but men never really grow up. They're taken care of by their mothers, their wives, their lovers. And then they have that strong male bonding to carry them through also. I say all this, but remain with men. They are a part of my life. And I plan to stay married. I believe in marriage because women alone in this society are treated like garbage. It's good to have a marriage when it works. It offers comfort and confidence. It's also good to have affairs provided one doesn't get too involved with the lovers. That's my philosophy."

Ambivalent about men, Cynthia has evidently been locked into relationships her entire adulthood. The attention and companionship of men continue to be important, although she also feels as if she's figured them out . She derives certain power from her experiences and her ability to recognize her needs. Cynthia's affairs with men have a hostile overtone. She seems to be working out her anger and disappointment with men through these various connections. She is also trying to bury her negativism by repeatedly seeking men, eventually leaving or disconnecting from them. It may be obvious to Cynthia that her solution to her ambivalence toward men hasn't worked out that well. It is for this reason that she repeats her actions over and over.

CRSO

Marsha

Marsha grew up in a small city in the Northeast and presently lives in a northeastern suburb. In her late thirties now, she describes her background as "very strict and patriarchal," having had the expectation that she would be married and lead a life similar to that of her parents. Feeling trapped before she began, at the age of twenty she was married for the first time, to a man who was several years older. Within two years they had a child.

"The marriage was warped from the start, very strange. Things occurred that I wasn't warned about, and I was too young to talk to anyone, to seek help. My husband and I never had sex. I had no idea why, but the rejection really damaged me. He'd never give me a straight answer but he'd tell me it wasn't my fault. Years later I learned he went elsewhere for sex, but at the time I didn't even know that. There was so much pain, loneliness and emptiness. I didn't even know where to turn."

After a year or so of this pattern, Marsha sought out other men.

"I began to go out. I'd go dancing at discos. I thought I was in love with whoever I slept with, because I'd been raised to think that. If you had sex with a man, it translated into love. My husband didn't mind my going out dancing, because I went with my sisters and their friends. I looked forward to those nights so much. They were my only form of escape."

Marsha met her first lover at a disco.

"He was Spanish, my age, single. I had a baby at home but all I could think about was this man. He was so very Latin—the accent, the liquor, the moves, the seduction. In retrospect, I understand that he really played up the part.

"I'd see him once a week and we'd dance and have sex. It was incredible, beyond my wildest imaginings. It became an obsession. If I couldn't see him, I'd flip. One time my husband was also going out and the sitter canceled. I almost had a nervous breakdown. Soon after that, I sneaked out on Friday night. My husband was at a stag party and my mother took the baby. I went to the disco and he was there, the Latin lover. We went right to his place and made passionate love. The sex was like nothing you could ever imagine. After coming from a passionless marriage, his passionate love and sex made me crazy. We did it everywhere, on the kitchen floor, the bathroom floor, against the wall, on the bed, off the bed… you name it. I was exhausted and exhilarated and sick to my stomach at the idea of it being six in the morning and needing to drive home to my husband. On the ride home, I kept remembering the six hours of solid lovemaking and my stomach churned at the thought of it. I lied to my husband and said I'd stayed at a friend's house. From that point on, the marriage fell apart."

By then Marsha was so absorbed with thoughts of this lover that she was unable to function.

"I was bumping into walls. All I did was think of my lover and when I'd next see him. Then I began to realize that it was my husband who had the problem, not me. If my lover would so readily and continually touch me, happily, then my husband was the one who didn't get it. But I was unable to confide in anyone, because my sisters and my mother would not accept what I'd done. So I was alone with my confusion. After two months of this, I told my husband we needed help. I saw my lover still but I couldn't keep up with the sex. I felt too guilty, yet I yearned for the sex and passion he offered. I was too frightened to sustain the love affair. And I learned that Latin men are very macho—so while he wanted me, when I turned away, despite his professions of love, he soon went on to the next woman. I was preoccupied with my marriage at that stage. I couldn't keep it together but we tried. We saw someone once or twice and got back together and then split up again. I heard that my husband also had a lover. It was the last straw. I began to take on other lovers and finally I separated from my husband.

"Then I had tons of lovers. My goal was to fill every sexual need I could possibly have. It became a sport for me. All I wanted to do was have sex with a man, no relationship beyond that. It was fun, a game. Sex in the ocean, on the beach, in the bathtub. I loved that I really used men. I was punishing them for my husband, and for my Latin lover. I definitely preferred younger men. Nineteen- or twenty-year-old boys were my favorite. The more they needed the experience, the more I taught them. I called them my 'little toys.' I never wanted to see them for anything but sex.

"During this period when I was having sex with lots of men, I never felt in my body. I was having a good time, but it was as if I was a spectator, as if it was happening to someone else. I was that detached. That way they couldn't hurt me. I very seldom had orgasms. But with my lover who became my second husband, I did, if we had oral sex. Maybe that's why I married him, because I was so bothered that I couldn't stay in my body. I couldn't feel anything emotionally, even with my lover who became my husband. I suffered from this. But I married him anyway because he came closer than the others.

"He was the only lover I lived with. I was married but left to live with this man. He is a few years younger than me. I liked the sex and he seemed to listen to me, he seemed to hear what I had to say when we were lovers. I have a theory that the first six months with a lover is show biz; all the good stuff is put forward. That was how I got hooked. By the second six months, all the garbage hung out and I asked him to leave. But we did marry. I was mistaken about him. I had a hunch that he was shallow, that I was getting myself into another bad scene, another bad marriage, but I went forward anyway. As my lover he was almost enough for me, but as my second husband, he wasn't deep enough. He offered no feedback. I thought I was in love with him, as I had thought with my first husband. I married him although I had doubts and we had a child immediately."

A year ago, Marsha's marriage to her second husband started to disintegrate. Six months ago she began to see another man.

"Last summer I ran into my high-school sweetheart. He was someone that everyone expected me to marry all along. In fact I'd broken his heart to marry my first husband. I'd heard that he married eventually and had a child. The minute I saw him, after all these years, I knew I'd divorce my second husband and marry him. So there we were, both married, with young children, and we began this amazing love affair. And when we had sex, I stayed in my body. It scared me how much I had loved him in high school—you know that kind of love. The love of my life. And here it is again, after a full circle and serious mistakes.

"I see this lover as much as possible. I wish we could be together twenty-four hours a day. And I never wanted to be with a man for any stretch of time before. This love affair is emotional and physical. We are totally connected. I'm not sure that marriage is in the picture, but I need to be with my lover, to share, to spend every moment with him. We talk about everything and I feel sharing with him. He won't use it against me. So I'm going to leave my present husband, who knows nothing about this, and start again. I believe that having married twice for the wrong reasons and brought two children into the world, I've finally figured it out. I'm hoping it will work this time, that, my self-searching has come full cycle."

Being married at twenty, with a child by the age of twenty-two, is notable in terms of having closed out adult opportunity. Marsha then grabbed on to the second marriage against her better judgment out of need to feel secure and anchored. She latched on to this man in order to be "set," and because she still suffered from low self-esteem. Thus her second marriage failed, as had the first.

We wait to see what happens with the fairytale aspect of her latest extramarital relationship. She appears to be more self-aware and in touch with herself now, a situation which positions her for a more positive result.

CRSO

Lilly

Lilly is forty-four years old and lives in northern California. She began her story by explaining that she came from an "extremely conventional" background and that she'd never been exposed to men until college. She is presently married and has two children, but the "road to normalcy" was filled with unexpected encounters.

"I lived with a man for many years. It was a commitment that I would describe as a marriage in every way, with the expectation of fidelity and loyalty. During this relationship I had two affairs. My 'live-in' never learned of the first, and the second was what destroyed us.

"My first affair was with a sixteen-year-old boy, if you can believe it. I was friendly with his mother and I still am, to this day. In a strange way, she was relieved that I was involved with her son. She was actually pleased about it. We lived in a small town and she worried about her sons. I represented someone who could talk sense into her son. So she condoned the affair, which lasted several months.

"There is nothing sexual about sex with a sixteen-year-old boy. They have orgasms in about a minute. There is no sexuality—all of it is beforehand, in the buildup. The sex itself is a letdown. But he was gorgeous and had a gorgeous physique. That was what appealed to me."

Lilly believes that the "taboo side" of an affair is what makes it attractive. She describes her connection to this young man as "totally unacceptable."

"I liked this titillating aspect, the dance beforehand, the unsanctioned bit; that had to be why I was there. I think the relationship had some comic aspects to it. It only lasted for several months because I got bored. I was his first older lover and I played the role well, and then it was time to finish it. I never considered the relationship to be motherly on my part. It wasn't a friendship; it was actually a curiosity. I admit that I'd been curious and it was interesting for me to see what it was all about. But I was constantly wondering if I'd end up hurting this person, if it was a negative situation for him. I felt guilty about having a lover to begin with, being in what was equivalent to a marriage, and then the age of this lover was constantly on my mind. He was the same age as my live-in's daughter. That was hard to handle.

"At the height of the relationship, he invited me to his high school graduation. No one knew we were lovers. So I was there as a family friend. Then we all went to dinner, my live-in, his daughter, my parents, his mother…it was wild. I realized then that it was absolutely absurd. It is one thing to reach for the unreality of a lover—but this was stretching it."

The next lover was Lilly's "nemesis," a relationship she has regretted ever beginning.

"Later on in the relationship with my live-in, I met another man.

He was more age-appropriate than my first fling and I was totally swept away. I was awed by how handsome he was. I was working in a restaurant, running the place, and I had noticed him when he came in several times before. This guy was single, which made him available. One night when my live-in wasn't around for some reason, we immediately got together. First we spoke at the bar and later we arranged to meet and ended up at my place.

"I didn't feel one iota of guilt about this. I was enthralled. I wouldn't do it now for a million dollars because it is so destructive to a marriage or a live-in relationship. I also can't imagine doing it today because I have children. At that stage I was intrigued with this man and I had to see it through. I saw him once a week for a few years and then I left my live-in to be with him. I think I superimposed my idea of a perfect relationship on him. As an affair it was very exciting. The sex was fabulous when we were in that stage because there was less to lose.

"Once I fell hopelessly in love with him, and it was more than an affair, it was a disappointment. I have a theory that these affairs work wonderfully as affairs but as relationships they rarely work. So I ended up with a great affair, a lousy relationship.

"I probably should have stayed only to see the affair to an end, but I was so taken with him. I left my live-in and he became the next relationship until my marriage. I would not have an affair now. I would not jeopardize my family. I've made a commitment now. What I see is how one fantasizes about these affairs, the sex and passion. I don't seem able to have that without loving someone, which means I fall in love and destroy whatever I already have. I recognize my pattern of not being able to detach my emotions from my sexuality. I have no regrets about the experiences but no desire to repeat them in any way. I think you have to have them to know what they are about, that's the catch. On the other hand, I have come amazingly close in an instance or two. I've stopped myself based on what I know and what I have today."

Lilly has learned a great deal from her affairs in terms of what she wanted and could manage with a spouse. She has utilized her affairs with men as a vehicle to understand men and to figure out what it is she wants for the long term.

When she attempted to transform her lover into her husband she was devastated by the result. The man she chose was not "husband material" and a tremendous letdown. Lilly saw the disintegration of the affair as a true loss of any potential rapport with this man. She was caught with rose-colored glasses on when she was immersed in the relationship with her lover. There is transference when one projects all her hopes and wishes and dreams onto another person. The hope then is that this one person can fulfill all those desires.

The disaster came about because Lilly was unable to work through her needs before she left her live-in lover. However, her present view of men and relationships has been altered so she has a better understanding of herself.

C3&O

Maryanne

Maryanne, who is in her late forties, tells us that her childhood consisted of a strict Catholic upbringing in the Southeast. One of six children, she was raised to marry and have children, while a career was never presented as important. She came to a northeastern city on business and was married at twenty-three. Continuing her work, she and her husband led a "sybaritic life," with the best of everything. Due to his work they traveled a great deal and put off having children. Not having children was an issue Maryanne struggled with.

"My husband never wanted to have children, from the start. And

I was in love with him, so to please him I resisted my own impulse to get pregnant. Eventually it became such an issue between us that he would leave me periodically to have extramarital affairs and then he'd return, apologetic. After several incidents of doing this, showering me with gifts and being remorseful, I got pregnant. By then I'd been married for a number of years."

When Maryanne's child was born, her husband left again. Although she began to "feel a loathing toward him" at this stage, she made the conscious decision to remain married and to keep her family intact.

"My background was one where no one left, no one destroyed a family. So while I barely tolerated his behavior while we were childless, I now had different considerations."

It was at this juncture that Maryanne met her lover. When her husband returned, she chose to "keep it up with her lover."

"He has been my lover throughout. I suppose it began as a revenge relationship, in order to get back at my husband. While I was certain that my husband never learned of the affair, I knew it was revenge anyway, an emotional revenge. And it felt good, emotionally and physically, to have this lover. I began to enjoy the relationship."

The lover comes from "another world" than the one Maryanne and her husband exist in. Ten years younger, he is relatively uneducated and is self-made.

"My husband was well educated and spoon-fed. This man works with his hands. It is a completely different head trip. I think it was the initial attraction, that he is so unlike Peter. I relish the uniqueness."

The sex has been a major component of the relationship since the start.

"Sex is fabulous. John is ten years younger and it's another experience altogether than being with my husband–I suspect with any husband, for that matter. I am always conscious that John is my lover, my young, sexy, handsome lover and I chose purposely to exude this sexuality. My husband had many affairs like this, in the name of sex and attraction, and I decided to have mine. I'm not ready to give it up, but I don't have any intention of marrying John and he is beginning to press me. I'm in it for the sex and the self-esteem that it provides. I especially needed the self-esteem after my husband went around blatantly cheating on me for years. It took a long while for me to feel desirable. John made a big impact. He treats me beautifully. And while not intellectually stimulating, he's a kind, attractive man who really cares about me."

Maryanne finds herself comparing her lover to her husband, even now that she is contemplating divorce.

"There is not one point of reference between the two men. And to this day it matters, even now that I've decided to leave my husband. For the many years I've spent with John while I was married to Peter, I have always understood it was an affair. In other words, in anticipating that I might get divorced one day, I never envisioned John as the alternative."

Maryanne has conducted the relationship with John from a "position of strength."

"As soon as we began our affair, I began to feel good about myself. And then I was able to relax, to accept the parts of the relationship that made me feel good. Mostly it was the sex. We share an incredible sex life.

"Although I no longer have to tiptoe about, I do remain careful not to have John sleep overnight because of my child. And there's one aspect of this that I appreciate, i.e., not having to wake up next to someone else. I did it in my marriage for so long and it didn't always feel great, so I'm in no rush to put myself in the same position. I like having my freedom, freedom to have John come and go as I choose, not as anyone tells me, not because we share a home and family. I think the main attraction is sexual.

"Now that I am healing from the pain of my marriage and I've renewed my self-confidence, this affair does not seem as critical to me."

Maryanne feels "grateful" to her lover, grateful for his attention and caring.

"Without him, I might never have recovered from the pain my husband inflicted. He was really a dreadful husband, who had many affairs and deceits. I think I'm frightened to go forward and marry again as a result of that. Then I think of John, who would only take care of me and protect me. Yet he's not the answer, although he's a great lover. I'm not quite ready to let it go."

The more salient point with Maryanne is how important the sexual aspect of the relationship was. Because she needed the affirmation, the affair was meaningful. Yet the liaison with her lover relates to her dissatisfaction with the marriage and her anger toward her husband. Maryanne does not compartmentalize the affair versus the marriage; this is not her need. Although the affair exists, her emotional life is wholly directed toward her husband. She is still fixated on him. While Maryanne is interested in her lover, it may appear that she is only interested in using her affair as a device to leave a bad marriage. In some ways the lover is incidental and she continues to have powerful feelings for her husband.

ೲ

Marla

Marla is forty-one years old and lives in Portland, Oregon. The oldest of seven children, with a mother who was married three times, Marla found herself in her first marriage at nineteen. She describes her mother as "a gorgeous woman who loved men and didn't care about her kids." Marla believes that her mother's behavior in terms of men has definitely affected her own attitude.

"I have been married twice. Both times I married for genetic reasons and I have two wonderful children, one from each marriage. My first husband was a scientist. He was very brainy and I was bored. After three years I had a major affair. I think it happened mostly because my husband was not a sexual draw, but emotionally and mentally it had worked for the most part. I never felt guilty because I'd give one hundred percent to this relationship and he had not given that back to me.

"The affair lasted for three years. We worked together, this man and I, which is how we met. I was very attracted to him. From the start we had sex, meeting at a hotel near the office. The affair ended up lasting for five years. I saw him daily at work and he became obsessed with me. We went to a hotel almost every day and ended up renting an apartment together. Both of us had young children when it began and were married."

When asked if her husband suspected anything, Marla replied that he had because of a letter found. Yet she continued the affair.

"It lasted because I felt better with this man. My marriage was so unhappy. I loved every single second of the relationship; that was what brought me happiness. My girlfriends knew about it and were in cahoots and helped me cover. They knew I was in a bad marriage and were pleased for me. I should have left the marriage but I needed a catalyst. When I finally left, I left for me, not for him. He left his wife for me, though. But it wasn't good enough, the setup with this guy. I loved him but I never could trust him because of our affair."

Marla did not sleep with her husband once the affair was in full swing.

"The affair began during a bad point in my marriage. I suppose I became obsessed after a time. The sex was great. It was the best I've ever had. We did everything. Everything in dirty movies, masturbation, drugs, we did it all.

"This lover left Portland to live in Washington for work. We'd been winding down for a while and we were both divorced by then. When I went to visit, he introduced me to his family and asked me to get married. I said yes and then when I returned home, I changed my mind. I suppose it was really the end, because he seemed to understand my decision. He fell in love with someone else soon after that. I was no longer in love with him or the relationship or whatever I'd been in love with. His asking me to marry him and to make a commitment had turned me off. Maybe it was too long after the passion of the affair. It was like the movie *Last Tango* in the sense that we really never knew one another as a couple."

At this time, Marla was divorced and began to date. She met her next husband almost immediately.

"This trip around I decided to like someone before I married him. I'd had a lot of boyfriends while I was divorced and I thought this man was the right choice.

"I was never in love with my second husband, nor had I been in love with the first. But my second husband was a decent, down-to-earth, very kind man. We had one child together and once again, I realized I'd married someone for genetic reasons. There I was with two smart children from two passionless marriages.

"At the same three-year point in this marriage, I got into a relationship again, using it as the catalyst to get out once more. I met a man from Los Angeles who was visiting in Portland and came to a party at my house. It was love at first sight. Again I had no guilt. By then I felt I'd given my marriage my best shot."

The lover who entered Marla's life during her second marriage was thirteen years younger than her, and she felt she was "out of control" in the circumstance.

"He moved into our house because he needed a place to live. By the second day we were on the floor. We did it against the washer and dryer. The sex was beyond belief. The best in the world. We did it on the train tracks, we did it in bars. He would masturbate me at a crowded bar. We did it in New York at Tavern on the Green, in the ladies' room. It was wild and highly sexual.

"During the first year and half, I was still married. I have to say that I became more obsessed with this man than with anyone I'd ever met. I didn't want to sleep with my husband once I began with my lover."

Marla's lover was involved with her children and family life because he lived in the attached apartment. The risks she was willing to take were notable.

"We'd take my kids to the zoo and do it in the car when the kids fell asleep. We had sex constantly. Constant, constant, constant sex. He was the one I was in lust with. I felt it was meant to be.

"The relationship faded after one particular episode. This man was very jealous and one night after I'd split from my husband, he climbed through the window at four in the morning because he was convinced that I was with someone. But I wasn't. By then he'd become demanding and I was on the road to being single again, so I broke it off. We did see one another a few times afterward and of course we made passionate love, but it was over. In my opinion, it didn't last because we never really liked each other. There was love maybe, lust definitely, but no liking. That's what doomed it."

Today, Marla feels that as a divorcee she is ready for an affair with a married man. She seems to view it as a new experience, a curiosity.

"I do have a serious boyfriend who I half live with but I'm conducting an affair with a married man. I think this is the next stage for me because it seems to be working. I was in New York recently and I met another married man there who I'm also beginning to see. I've never pursued attached men before, purposely, so I find it intriguing.

"I think it would be best to be married again, this time to someone wealthy, and I don't intend to cheat. Whatever I am, whoever I am, I would love someone to love me and to be real and human. I want someone to want me for myself. If that can happen then I'll love that person until the day I die and I'll never ever wander."

Maria is very like her mother, whom she describes at the beginning of the interview, although she might not be aware of this similarity.

Sex is a very important issue for her, as is having smart children. Marla splits herself often in order to hold on to both parts of her life. She has strong beliefs about men, her main idea being that one type of man is for procreation, the other for sex.

While her story is exciting and action-filled, it is clear that Marla has struggled with her attachments to men.

CR&O

Helen

Helen, who lives in Chicago, sees herself as a strong, principled forty-five-year-old mother of two teenagers. Her marriage is a "very happy" one, although she believes that she was married too young. Helen has conducted several romances outside her marriage

"In the early years of my marriage, we were in the army. I was away from my family and I no longer had to be the 'good little girl' they saw me as. Maybe I married before I had a chance to discover my sexuality or maybe I somehow became a different person than I'd been before I left the country. Whatever it was, I ended up having a series of lovers. I suppose I saw this as an opportunity to be wild and I had this sensation that I might never have the opportunity again. So, I took advantage of it and I learned a lot."

Her first lover was another army member.

"He was an unmarried American man. I would see him in between projects, when I had little to do. During the projects themselves, I would work until I was exhausted, and there was no time for any kind of extramarital relationship. It was the down time that pushed me toward other men. With this lover we'd meet to collaborate on projects. That was an excuse that worked and no one questioned the situation for one moment. He lived in a rural area; it was wild and beautiful. We made love in these incredible jungle settings, sometimes by waterfalls. I would describe this affair as very romantic and scenic. I was caught up in the whole picture, where we were, the feeling it evoked."

Sometime later she met a high-level government official of the country where she and her husband were stationed. Although they did not connect immediately, Helen began to see him while doing a report on his department.

"He invited me to dinner after a meeting. We saw each other several times after that before it became sexual. He was older and a most accomplished lover. I was acutely aware of the fact that having an affair with a married woman was not new to him. Yet I liked how he treated me. What he taught me. He kept a splendid apartment in the capital of this country so he was not with his family when he was there on official business. He had time and the freedom to become involved with many women. I was attached to this lover for different reasons than my American lover. He was foreign and exciting. It was quite something to be with both men at once. To keep it quiet and to keep the marriage going was another feat."

Helen conducted the affair with both men simultaneously for a period of time before moving back to the States.

"Once we returned, I swore to myself that I'd never again get involved with a man outside my marriage, that I'd commit to the marriage. But back in Chicago I began to conduct several affairs. By then I suspected that my husband was doing his own thing, having his own affairs. I was busy with my life and did not pay much attention to his, at that point. I was too busy with my liaisons to care. My marriage had another dimension, the one that incorporated my lovers."

Twice a year, Helen's first lover from the army would visit, now that he was living in California.

"Because he was a family friend, he would be our house guest. But we were still involved with each other and every visit we rented a hotel room in town for the afternoon. We were desperately afraid that my husband would catch us together. We were so worried that we took a different route back to the apartment in separate cars. Then we'd all go out to dinner. Occasionally, my lover would even bring a date. It was worth it for me, the risk, the attachment to this man, the charade with my husband."

Helen's "escapades" ended when she realized what appealed to her the most: a home, a family, and children.

"I think about what I was like when I was first married and when my children were small. What seemed like a trap then now seems to be substantial and important. That was the end of my roving. But I have a scrapbook of my days in the army when my lovers were most thrilling to me. I watch my children as they admire the pictures, especially as I stand in photographs with each of my lovers."

Helen represents traditional values. She values both her marriage and her children but is driven to these other men primarily to seek sexual satisfaction. She seems almost proud of her relationship with other men. The sex was important but she wanted to maintain the conventional aspects of her life.

৫৪০

Linda

Linda is approaching forty and lives in Boston. She was married in her mid-twenties and the marriage lasted ten years. Her childhood was "happy and predictable" and she believed that she was "imitating" it when *she* married and had children.

"I became involved with a man who summered at the same place. We had mutual friends but I realized that I had nothing in common with his wife as early as when it was an innocent social setting. But I always liked him. I had known him for a few seasons at the beach when the affair began. Our spouses had gone back to Boston for the week and we met for coffee. We talked and then arranged to meet in another town for dinner.

"The sex began soon after. I felt very guilty. I had small children and my marriage wasn't bad; it just lacked passion. That's why I latched on to this–there was passion in this. At the beginning of the relationship I think I was bored and unhappy, and I didn't look to mend the marriage but instead I found this distraction. Then I became really wrapped up in the affair and I ran from the marriage. All the time I was freaking out."

The intensity of the relationship was something that Linda found difficult to balance.

"It began to get hot and heavy. I was running to pay phones to make calls to him. We'd meet for an hour here and there, whatever we could manage. There were excuses and lies. I felt I was leading two lives and it was horrible. Then I think we both fell in love. What happened was that I loved my husband but I really wasn't in love with him. For a year our relationship wasn't physical, a symptom of something wrong. Instead of facing it, instead of examining our marriage, I was preoccupied with the affair. It was definitely all-consuming. I'd meet him at horrid hotels so we wouldn't be seen by anyone. I was tortured by the guilt. There was guilt for my kids, for my husband, for breaking up the marriage.

"Then on weekends we'd see each other as couples and act as if nothing was going on. He and I orchestrated these social engagements so we could be together."

Linda's tryst remained a secret for six months before it was discovered.

"Things deteriorated because I found the duality too difficult to handle, and I provoked a separation from my husband. My husband tried to hold on to the marriage. I didn't realize how serious the situation was. I thought I'd go from one marriage directly to another. My lover and I had talked about being together. It was understood we'd be leaving our spouses for one another. But he was evasive about marriage and I didn't pay enough attention. I would not have left my marriage if I'd known that he wouldn't marry me. I didn't realize the ramifications. What I realized from the extramarital relationship was how empty and passionless my marriage was. I was the catalyst for him to leave a bad marriage, a marriage in worse shape than mine.

"Friends perceived me as brave to leave a marriage that was lacking. But I only did it for this man. I wanted to leave, but I looked around and said to myself I was no less unhappy than my friends. I left because I became obsessed with him. It became a physical thing and I was convinced I was in love."

Linda describes the sex as "compelling."

"I know that some women have affairs only for the sex. I should have played out the sex before I left my marriage. I should have had the affair and not destroyed my marriage. I was too taken over by the affair as I waited to see what happened next. I watched myself separate from my husband and my lover separated from his wife. Then I was with him constantly. We began to see one another every night. There I was juggling my kids while my marriage was breaking up and I was having sex with my lover."

During this period, Linda and her lover comforted one another.

"We were fighting with our spouses and so we relieved and consoled one another. I think that the unreality of an affair is how you make your home life worse and then you run to each other for comfort.

"He and I each divorced our spouses, which took years, and we remained together. It was the beginning of the end, though, once we were divorced. My divorce came through first and I sensed his insecurity. Then his divorce came through and he backed off. I panicked as we adjusted the relationship, without any plans of marriage. I thought I wanted to marry him but I started to see character traits. I stayed with him out of confusion. I'd given up so much for him, I couldn't say he wasn't worth it and admit my mistake. Finally I left. I'm only sorry that I stayed for as long as I did. I am regretful that the affair ever happened or that I didn't examine the situation in a different way. I don't think I knew myself well enough and I was looking for a man to make me happy. I now understand affairs and marriage better and I wouldn't make that same mistake again."

Linda was vulnerable to the relationship with her lover because she felt that her marriage lacked passion. She attempted to escape the boredom of it and became caught up in the love affair. The affair was very disappointing and she had to regroup. Linda apparently struggled from the get-go with an extramarital affair. Her expectations were not met after leaving the marriage in hope of marrying her lover.

ভেরে

Julie

Julie is from Dallas and now lives in a nearby suburb. She is forty-one years old and has just recently remarried. Her first marriage lasted over twelve years and it was during this period that she encountered her lover.

"My first marriage was problematic. The first few years were fine, and then my husband became a manic-depressive and lost all interest in sex, in our child, in our life together. After several terrible years, I ran into a friend from my childhood, someone who had been my boyfriend when we were practically children. It was an old emotional link, but it still existed. He was married at the time but we were both interested.

"We began to have lunch together and he showed me the attention I needed. Soon enough we began a love affair. Although we were very careful to conceal the relationship because we knew so many people in common, I had difficulty keeping up the facade. I was confused about my emotions. After a day with my lover I'd return home feeling very uncomfortable and the deceit was difficult. I worried I'd get caught; mostly I worried because I didn't want to give up my lover."

Julie describes the sex as "great."

"The sex was hot and heavy, very passionate. On Wednesdays I was off from work and we'd spend the entire day in bed at a motel. We did it for hours, having intercourse three times at least. He was very attentive and caring. He took his time and was interested in satisfying me. We never rushed through it. It was wonderful and I realized how unlike a marriage it was. Every aspect of our time together was important. I became obsessed with him and thought of him all the time. I'd drop my kid at religious school and rush to see him for an hour. We'd stay up all night sometimes, making love and drinking wine.

"My self-esteem had been low, due to a bad marriage. Then he came along. I was told I was sexy, beautiful and smart. I felt like a woman again. I began to realize that I needed a lot from a man that I wasn't getting from my husband. Intimacy, communication, sex–I got it all from my lover.

"I began to identify myself as a sexual being; that was a big deal to me. He really brought me back to life and I no longer felt repressed. When your husband tells you you're no good, over and over, you begin to believe it. This lover made all that disappear. And I loved the glamour of it, not just being a housewife and a mom, but having a lover with a secret world. We fulfilled each other's fantasies for a long time. That was a big part of it."

The relationship lasted several years, and finally Julie decided to get divorced. At the same time, her lover sought a divorce and although they still continued to see one another, they ultimately chose other partners for their second marriages.

"I definitely loved him, but the timing was never right. And then there was the question of trust. The trust was missing, because after all, we'd cheated on our spouses for each other. How could we trust each other if put in a position? I wondered about it often. I was afraid to be locked into a relationship which had begun as ours had. And I needed more than a predominantly sexual relationship for the long term. Yet he was so special to me. I always thought of how much we cared when we were young, and I believe we'll always care on some level. But we treated one another badly after a few years—we were insanely jealous. And I think he felt that once I decided to get divorced, I favored my daughter over him. It wasn't the case, but the nature of the relationship had changed and couldn't sustain itself. Once we were no longer illicit lovers and reality set in, we didn't function as well."

Still, Julie looks back fondly on her relationship with her lover.

"I owe him a great deal. He precipitated my request for divorce and gave me the confidence to do it. It was only in my involvement with him that I realized how much was missing from my life, how unsatisfied I was. I'd been so afraid of being out there alone and independent. But this lover made me feel good enough about myself and my own sexuality that I was able to make the break.

"I was able to begin a new life. I'm happily married today and would no longer pursue an extramarital affair. I wouldn't risk it as

I'd been willing to risk it in the past. If you want an end to a marriage, an affair is one method of effecting it, I think. I no longer have the desire."

Julie benefited from her affair. It gave her the courage to leave an unhappy situation. The sex and attention her lover gave her at a low point in her life helped to build her up. Then she was ready to go ahead. It was as if she was fortified by what took place in the relationship with the lover.

The lack of trust which Julie describes has been mentioned by other interviewees. The premise that they and their lovers shared a deceit while involved in an affair seems acceptable. However, once they face convention, i.e., marriage to the lover, women such as Julie often question how they can trust this partner as a spouse. After all, Julie's lover was unfaithful to his wife for Julie's sake. What will he do to Julie as his wife for his lover's sake? And how will she observe the tradition of fidelity with a lover turned husband?

CRARO

Charlene

Charlene, who is in her forties, is from Virginia and has lived in Los Angeles for most of her adult life. She comes from an "uncomplicated" family and is one of three sisters. She describes her first marriage as "doomed from the start."

"I really didn't want to get married but I saw all my friends getting married and I felt that I had no choice. I really did not know what my alternatives were. I used my husband as a vehicle to get out of my life. When we moved to L.A., my husband worked long, odd hours and he was never around. I hated the city and there I was, completely on my own. My husband asked his friend who was still single to sort of take care of me and show me around. For a period of time his friend did just that, and then it became an affair."

Charlene was "undeniably attracted to this man."

"He was a little man who drove a Porsche and had money. He was very L.A. I liked that because it wasn't my background. I was infatuated with his lifestyle. I was turned on to the whole picture. My lover seemed to be so much more sophisticated than my husband and I also liked that.

"The sex was much freer because he wasn't my husband. I'm convinced that sex is much more exciting when you're sneaking it. You get pumping before you even begin. We'd go to his apartment when my husband thought he was showing me a good time and we'd be having this amazing sex together.

"I think the sex with this man, without thoughts of one's day-to-day existence, made it thrilling. There is no mortgage, no car, no kids, no alarm clock at 6 AM with a lover. Another aspect of the relationship was that I was so inexperienced. So when I started having sex outside my marriage, it was like someone had pushed a button. A whole new vista opened up for me. I was really turned on to this guy. He was on my mind constantly; I thought about it all the time.

"Either I was absolutely in love with him or I believed that being in love makes it okay. I never knew there was such a thing as being in lust. I didn't understand. Everything we did together was special, and had an aura about it. We went to dinner; he took me to wonderful places and to jazz clubs. We did all the things together that my husband wasn't available to do. I think I got confused about who I was married to. My husband had married me in good faith and there I was, with his best friend. It wasn't his fault.

"If anyone was at fault, it was my lover. He came on to me. In retrospect, where was he in that he came on to someone else's wife? Maybe everything was competitive for him and it reached as far as his best friend's wife."

Charlene was vocal about her plans to leave her husband for her lover but admits that he "never committed himself."

"But he didn't discourage me, either. He simply listened. He knew I disliked my marriage. Maybe he considered his role to be the catalyst to set me free. I'm not sure what he had in mind.

"I do know, however, that he opened my eyes. I remember that growing up we were taught that men were a game and catching them was the name of the game. We would say things to our friends like 'I got him' or 'I won.' This was a hopeless game to me and sex never came into it. It was taboo. Sex as sport was left for men only. Later on I realized I could like men, once I was on my own. I look at the relationship with my lover as something he instigated but since it set me free, it worked out fine. Once I was divorced I called my lover thinking we'd be together. He said to me, 'I wouldn't date my best friend's ex-wife.' That was it for me. I had to move on."

Charlene is no longer interested in conducting an extramarital affair.

"A penis is a penis. After a while it's the relationship that makes the difference. A zipless fuck begins to wear thin and it all begins to feel the same after a while. I'm remarried now and have a truly solid marriage, but that's only because after my first lover and the subsequent divorce I had enough lovers to understand what I want and that sex is sex. Sex in long-term relationships has more to do with what you think of the relationship than it does with pure sex. While I learned a lot from my first lover, I wouldn't jeopardize my second marriage for that kind of experience."

Charlene seems to have learned from her lover how to move forward in her life. She realized what she would and would not do in a marriage as a result of her affair. In this sense she begins without much self-awareness and finishes with a heightened sense of self. Sex, however, was a major part of the love affair. It was exciting, stimulating, and she became uninhibited with it.

CR&O

Rachel

Rachel is fifty years old and lives in a suburb in the Southeast. She has been married for over twenty years to a man who is three years younger than her. She described her husband as someone she would never leave for another man, although she admits to "not loving him."

Her initial encounter with her lover occurred at a country club.

"Groups of us would go out together and if we weren't at the club we'd entertain each other at our homes. Always it was the same set of people. There was one husband in particular who was very handsome—incredibly handsome. We'd all whisper about him as if we were in high school. We asked his wife, who was very plain, if she didn't think he was gorgeous. I often wondered if this man's wife even took note of what a woman's man he was.

"Anyway, he was the prize and I was obsessed with him. I certainly had no romantic attachment; it was almost like a girlish crush. Then one night at a party he asked me to dance and while we were dancing I could feel how hard he was. That was the beginning. Sometimes my husband and I went out with him and his wife, the four of us or six of us in the same car, and he'd choose to sit next to me. By then it was a big deal in my life. I knew I wanted to sleep with him. That was my main preoccupation."

During this time, Rachel tells us, her husband noticed no difference in her behavior. She was quite aware of her looks and appearance and made "as many dates as possible" with the crowd that included her lover.

"I don't believe either of us was thinking clearly. He would have his hands all over me and we'd be driving down a dark street and my husband was sitting right there and so was his wife. It was daring and sexy, as if we existed without the others, regardless of their presence. In this world where the only important idea was to go to bed with him, I waited. The flirtation and attraction went on for months. We never discussed it but the tension was there.

"After dancing together at parties and at the club, one evening we escaped to the shed by the golf course and he went down on me. I wanted to believe that no one noticed that we were gone, but the truth was, it didn't matter. I only wanted to have sex with him. The rest faded into oblivion—all rational thought, all caution.

"After that he made it clear that he wanted me. I arranged it so that there was an empty place to go to. I lied to my husband and I lied to my friends and so it began. The time I spent with this man was passion beyond belief. I'd never had sex in my life like I had with him; it was everything I expected and hoped for. And I had no regrets."

Eventually Rachel's lover became uninterested in her, and she was baffled by his reaction.

"It was as if he wanted the chase and the catch but soon after, he let it go. I was disappointed because while it was going on, I felt young and secretive and sexy. I'm not happily or unhappily married, and I really wanted the sensation of being swept away. I wasn't going to run off with this man—that wasn't what it was about. It was absolutely physical and I loved that part. I was totally absorbed in it. When it was over, I tried to hold on and then I realized that I had to resume my life."

Rachel confided in one friend who, she says, "egged" her on.

"Every time I called my friend to tell her what happened, she'd be so supportive, so interested. It was as if what I did enhanced the everyday existence we all lead. She understood it wasn't a love affair, but simply an affair, based on sex, and she seemed to think that was fine. The intrigue and secrecy seemed the most beguiling part of it all.

"I have no regrets except that it didn't last longer. When we had sex together, he was able to have orgasms several times, and that was such a departure from my marriage. I felt young and alive. And

I knew good sex because I had been promiscuous before I got married. I recognized the real thing. He was absolutely magnificent. It was a relationship based on incredible sex."

When asked if she was disappointed that he no longer wanted the relationship, Rachel tells us:

"If I had been emotionally attached to him, I would have been distraught. But because I understood what it was from the start, I was able to accept the end. Of course, it was a rejection, and that always hurts, but there was not an emotional bond.

"I think as women get older, the opportunity to have an affair lessens and the younger women step up in place. That someone so handsome and so wonderful as a lover would choose me was quite a boost. I am thrilled to have experienced the sex and glamour of it. It added so much to my days. And I'm relieved it was nothing more, no complications."

The sex for Rachel was important and came at a time in her life when she needed to feel desirable. It was an ego boost and she understood it to be that. She had no expectations of it going further and accepted it for what it was. Because she could appreciate this relationship on its own terms, it worked well for her.

൦ൽൽ

Alex

Alex is forty-eight years old and lives in New England. She has two teenage children and is presently divorced after a marriage that lasted for twenty-one years. Her previous marriage, when she was nineteen years old, was annulled. She describes her childhood as "abusive." Her father physically abused her and her mother sexually abused her when she was a very young child. Verbal abuse was instigated by her mother as well. Alex, after "years of therapy," believes there were "no boundaries" with her father. While he flirted there was no sexual abuse. She agreed to be interviewed because she wants to reach out to "someone else in pain."

"I was first married to get out of the house. I was only nineteen years old and he was twenty-four. He was extremely handsome, which mattered at the time. I felt so small and insignificant that the fact that someone like this man chose me was a boost to my self-esteem. But he was abusive too. He beat me up and fooled around. He came from a completely different background and he did not treat me as I expected he would. This marriage was annulled and I moved to New England within three weeks of the annulment.

"I had to make a living in the city. In those days a woman was defined by who she was with, not who she was. So my purpose was to be married again, to have children and to do it better than my mother."

Alex met her second husband when she was twenty-five and they were married within six months' time.

"He was socially acceptable and from my background. Despite how my parents had been, I needed to please them, always. And this choice was one they were pleased with. My husband lived in the city and soon after we had children. At the point in time when I married him, he was the best I could do. I loved him at first but as I grew older and began to experience life a bit, and got out there, I realized there was more. Ironically my husband was the one who gave me the courage to do it. The feedback from him was different than from the people. While he was a controlling man who wouldn't let me work, he was supportive in other ways. It was my children who helped me to grow up."

Men, Alex explains, have "always come on" to her, and when her youngest child was a baby, she noticed the man she would later want as her lover.

"I must play a part in how men approach me, but I'd never gone for someone else. When I saw this man on the tennis court at the club we joined, I told my friend, if ever I screwed around, I'd choose him. But I let the thought go for a while because I was afraid the marriage would be over if I fooled around. I'd been unhappy for years, but I was afraid to leave. How lucky I was to have this husband, I told myself. I was in my thirties with children and a husband. What more could I want?

"A group of us at the club all became friendly. He and his wife were a part of it. He was five years older than me, but very immature. Over a period of time, he and his wife and my husband and I became very friendly. I respected his wife but I never really liked her. I was discontent and didn't understand what was wrong with me. My husband fed into it. In retrospect, I see that my husband began to make money, which made him flirtatious. He began to feed his ego. I was extremely jealous. I definitely cared about my husband still and needed his approval. Then we took a summer house and so did this couple. Then we spent time together as couples. My husband idolized this man and I needed him, that side of him that nurtured me."

By then Alex was spending time with the other man.

"One day we went out shopping and he tried to kiss me. I pushed him away. I also rejected his next overture. The third time was a romantic dinner alone together and we began to date. We didn't sleep together but we kept it a secret from our spouses at that time anyway. We'd go to Staten Island and the Palisades. We'd go where no one would find us. Eventually we went to a hotel and were petrified. The second time it was for real and then it became an ongoing thing. We kept it very quiet and saw each other as often as possible. This began twelve years ago and is still going on."

Throughout the affair, until Alex's divorce, Alex and her lover saw each other with their spouses, as couples.

"We continued to socialize. It was a way of seeing him at first.

Then I wanted to have him all to myself. I fantasized. There was nothing real about him. I didn't want to face what he couldn't give me. He was pure fantasy for me. I'd escape from my husband and children whenever I needed to. I'd sit in the car on family trips and be with my lover in my mind.

"As it got going, the sex happened whenever we got together. Sex was unbelievable from the start and is even better today. We've grown in terms of what the relationship is. I used to ask about his wife, if he loves her. He told me that they have an arrangement. I never asked him to leave her; I know they have common goals. Yet I fantasized about what it would be like to be married to him. I don't think it would work because part of him is unemotional and cold."

During her marriage, Alex never asked her lover for anything because she was petrified of his rejection.

"It was his call or I thought I'd be left alone with my husband. I felt I was leading two lives and handling it very well. However, there is a tremendous amount of anxiety in an affair. Being absolutely secretive, the juices begin to flow. I think an affair can keep a woman in a marriage. I did break up with my lover in order to face my marriage but in the end I went back to him. My lover kept me there. Ten years ago I asked my husband for a divorce but he was immobilized by the request. So I stayed, and the affair secured the marriage."

"I didn't sleep with my husband for the last seven years of the marriage because he was hostile and jealous of any attributes I had. So I got even with him by withholding sexually. But the attraction to my lover was incredible. Before he'd ever touched me, and even more so once the affair began, there was an electricity about it, about being together. I think the electricity was telltale. People knew despite our secrecy. I used to tell myself, in another life we'll be together."

Last year Alex decided to leave her husband.

"I told my lover I was divorcing my husband. He asked me why and I asked him if he was going to disappear then, once I was single. He was quite struck by my decision. In our long-term relationship, we'd often spoken of our kids, but not our spouses. Yet he knew I was unhappy in my marriage. I think my deciding to leave was a courageous thing. My lover stayed with me, which made me happy. I needed him as I left a twenty-year marriage. To have lost a twelve-year lover at the same time would have been devastating."

Moving onward, Alex would "love to meet other men."

"I do not want to stop the affair but I believe it will be over at a stage when it gets in the way of my meeting someone else. If he left his wife I would like to date him. I wouldn't marry him without dating. Our lives are so separate. We don't go out alone together, to ball games, to movies. It's all secretive. There's nothing real about an affair. You can't be whoever you want to be with a lover. Instead you close that door. Maybe I hate the men I've known. They've been overrated and disappointing. I thought I loved my lover at the start but I do not. I haven't quite worked everything out enough to leave, though, but I'm getting there.

"If someone came to me I'd tell them not to have an affair in the same set of circumstances I was in. If I had faced the real issues of a bad marriage, I'd be somewhere else today. It took a long time but I feel terrific now."

Alex's story provides a happy ending in the sense that she has overcome a great deal. Evidently she had a very difficult, probably traumatic childhood but was able to find her way in the world. Through a meaningful affair she was able to learn a great deal about herself and her needs vis-à-vis men.

Yet Alex is not necessarily looking to turn the lover relationship into a marriage. She does, however, keep the possibility open. Her maturity is evident, emotionally and sexually speaking, in the relationship with her lover. The connection to her husband on these levels has simultaneously stagnated.

When Alex speaks of the socializing with her lover and his wife, it appears she is in denial about her anxiety. Also, the issues of what her lover's wife meant to her came to the surface. Her feelings of nervousness were genuine, and she used denial as a means to cope with the situation.

ↄ঩঵

Karen

Karen lives in a city on the East Coast, where she grew up. Her childhood was "normal and happy" and she was encouraged to attend college. Today she has been married for fifteen years and has three children. Excluding one brief period, Karen has maintained a full-time career throughout her marriage and childbearing years. Her marriage is "excellent" and her husband is a "good provider." Her association with other men began ten years ago, when she turned thirty.

"I guess it was because I was thirty. I began to think about other men. It was for the most basic of reasons: it was for sex. Although the sex was okay with my husband, I wanted to explore. The first time that I had an affair was when I was traveling for work. The lover was a bit older than me, actually my husband's age, and the episode occurred in another city. The relationship lasted six months, always taking place in this other city where I traveled for work. Whenever I was there I saw him."

Although Karen experienced some guilt, she "quickly got over it."

"I was definitely sleeping with two men at once. Again I was only initially bothered by such a concept and then I moved with it. I look at what I do as something that men have always done. Why not women? I have been at dinner parties where people discuss affairs. It's always more serious when a woman does it and only a slap on the wrist when a husband does it. I don't get it.

"My involvements with other men are only physical. Since I began I have had approximately eight lovers. Most of these attractions have not lasted long because I tire of them. I have only chosen them for sex and while the same applies to my present lover, he has lasted for over eighteen months and I cannot see giving this guy up.

Karen's husband has no idea of her trysts with other men, and she plans to keep it that way.

"I do love my husband. What I do with other men exists on another level. I would never think of leaving my husband for this lover or for any previous lover or for any future lover. I don't believe that my husband has anyone else. I'd feel terrible if he did. I'd be jealous, all the normal feelings. I'd wonder how I compared to other women he chose because I am constantly comparing him to the men that I'm with. I would worry about the emotional tie he might have with another woman. That would be unbearable for me.

"My present lover is eleven years younger than I am. It's a very convenient setup for both of us. I'm safe, he's safe from commitment. And healthwise too. We both have taken HIV tests and we are careful, very careful. We're both protected. Because I only have one lover at a time, and use condoms, I feel there is control in terms of STDs. I have a rule: it's a condom or no sex, if in a spontaneous situation. That's how it has to be."

Once Karen began her affairs, there were periods when she did not pursue anyone.

"Then I realized it's something I like to do. I like meeting my lovers at their places and I like it to be about sex, only. The lover I have now has a very large penis and while the myth says it doesn't matter, it does matter to me. The sex in this affair is what keeps it going. It is the most amazing ever. Whenever I've been with a lover, I've had sex that goes on and on, but nothing like this. I have noticed the difference between a clitoral orgasm and a vaginal orgasm. With lovers, especially my latest lover, I attain both.

"Although this lover and I are friendly, it certainly isn't my goal to have a conversation. I see him every week, and it varies as to what time of day. Sometimes I can see him at night and sometimes during the day."

Karen kept a journal of her times spent with her lovers.

"When I realized it was going to become a pattern, I decided to write it down to read in my rocking chair in my old age. Writing about it was a way to become at peace with myself. I began to understand why I do it. I do it for the excitement and the sex.

"It's nice to remember how I met these lovers. Mostly it was traveling for work. I noticed that when I began, the men were my age or older, and in the last few years they've become younger. As a woman approaches her forties, I think, and wants to have an affair, it should be with a younger guy. It's great for the ego and for the sex.

"The sex with most of my lovers has been much more exciting than the sex in the marriage. It's not only exciting but different and lasts longer. The sex with my latest lover is in a class by itself. I know the volume of orgasms is much greater with my lover than with my husband."

The lover and Karen met during a meeting for work and were very attracted to one another.

"We had a few lunches and then it started. It seems like when I was his age, twenty-nine, the men didn't look like that. The sex we have is fantastic. He has a wonderful body and is very handsome. He's very different from my husband physically. He's quite well hung and much more youthful. It's the physical part that keeps it going and I do it for me. I feel no guilt; I only worry about if it ends. I'd be crushed if this lover ever got married and left."

Karen believes that every woman should have this kind of experience.

"I can't imagine giving up this guy. He's pretty addictive. With other lovers I'd gone to hotels and I'd understood there was an end in sight. With this lover we are only at his place and it's so sexy I can't describe it. I do things with him I'd never do with my husband–never. We try everything, we do it eight and ten times a night. I think of him when I'm having sex with my husband. I think about him a lot of the time."

Karen is "very comfortable" with her lover and views the relationship as something "very special."

"I don't believe there should be this double standard. I think so many married women are conducting affairs, more than they admit. I know a man who calls himself a masseur, who certainly gives more than a massage to women; most are married. These women are really looking for sex. If and when this relationship ends, I will find another lover. It's a part of my life I won't give up."

Karen is a bit different because she is committed to loving multiple lovers. It seems that her interest is primarily in a variety of continual sexual experiences.

She uses denial and splitting as a method of conducting this other life. Essentially Karen's needs are sexualized. What makes her life interesting and exciting has to do with her sex-driven affairs. They are important to her on that level. Her sexuality drives the relationships.

ॐ

Monica

Monica, who is thirty-six, has been married since she was twenty. She grew up in Minneapolis–St. Paul in a family she describes as "typical blue collar." Monica married to "break free" of her family. For the last fourteen years of her marriage, she has been engaged in extramarital relationships.

"I suppose that I began because my husband is very detached and unfriendly. I found that he never thought I was pretty or attractive and while I might be average looking, it mattered to me very much that he thinks I look good. Other men I'd meet responded to me.

"I have been a dispatcher for a bus company for the last twelve years and I've been working with men for that amount of time. I look for men through my work and I always choose someone who is younger and unattached. Since I began, I have never been without a lover. It has become a part of my life."

Monica's husband has no idea of what is going on with her relationships outside the marriage. Because she has no intentions of leaving the marriage, she keeps it this way.

"I am now seeing a man who is twenty-six years old and works for the company. He drives a bus and is single. My lovers are always single. I purposely do it that way so there is no difficulty in beginning and ending the relationships. When the relationship gets serious, I immediately end it. I'm not there for anything but the sex and the feedback. I guess I do not want any messy business and I don't want another attachment. That is why I leave. Often these men seem to latch on to me, but it's not what I'm looking for."

Monica has no desire to jeopardize her marriage for her connections with other men.

"I have been doing this long enough to get the hang of it. I have a sense of who will work out and who is only going to be a sticky situation. Still, I have never been without a lover, and I suppose it's because I'm egotistical. But at least I understand what I'm in it for.

"My newest guy is someone I can see after work. I am able to tell my husband that a group of us from work are going out, and in fact we do. Afterwards, I meet my lover. Because I find single guys, they usually have their own place and that makes it easy. We have sex and I like it better than sex with my husband. The sex with these guys is important to me. I need that in the affair."

Monica says, however, that she avoids getting "hooked" on one man through sex.

"I would avoid any attachment at all, including sex. For me, the variety is what makes it work. I'm there for the experience and to see how they like me, how they appreciate me. After this lover, the bus driver, is over, I will go on to the next.

"I think I've figured it out now, how to find someone and not be at risk. I won't leave my marriage and I wouldn't put my marriage at risk, either. I think of my children and that they need healthy parents. What I do with other men is something only for me. It really doesn't spill over to my married life or to my role as a parent. I need it for myself. It only has to do with me."

Monica is intriguing in that she has a simplified system for herself. She has figured out what men are going to suit her needs as a lover and sexual partner. What Monica does is make calculated efforts to achieve these goals. She finds that this system, which she has smartly established, works positively for her.

&

Chelsea

Chelsea is thirty years old and was married for ten years. Divorced today, she has two children, lives in Cleveland, Ohio, and works full-time. Her childhood was intact, and it came as a surprise to her that she would have a "rocky" marriage, one that failed to meet her expectations. After two years of married life, Chelsea began to look to other men.

"I married for sex and then it stopped working. We were married for two years when I had my first affair. By five years into the marriage, I'd had a few affairs and I began to realize that the marriage sucked. I thought the affairs might be nice, might be a way of getting some relief for me.

"The first time, I went out for drinks with two girlfriends. I met a man. I don't think that he was married. One thing led to another and soon I was seeing him as much as I could. The relationship was based on sex. He was drop-dead, gorgeously handsome. Blue eyes, very tall, like my husband, broad and very similar. There has been a similarity to my husband in every lover I've ever chosen."

The first affair lasted several weeks and Chelsea felt guilty throughout the episode, even as it "launched her career."

"I ended it because I was too guilty. I'd meet him downtown at a bar and we'd go to my house because my husband wasn't there. I didn't think he'd show up, either. I wasn't worried about it, let's put it that way. I had a yes/no attitude about getting caught. I stopped sleeping with my husband while I was with this lover. I couldn't handle both men at once. The guy was an idiot but the sex was great.

"While I was feeling guilty about my husband I went on vacation and met someone else. That was my second fling. I want to explain that I'm not a tramp by any means, but my marriage was in deep trouble and my husband was boring, boring, boring.. Plus he had women on the side, throughout the marriage. I suppose because he had other women I was acting out against him."

The "weekend fling" which Chelsea had while on vacation was someone she knew she'd never see again. She lied about her name and who she was, and about the fact that she was married.

"The sex was very good but not great. He was sweet and tender but not passionate like my first lover. I was just getting started at that point. It was after this man that I met someone else, someone I began to spend some time with. He was a lover who lasted several months. His name was Ryan and he was someone I met at a party.

Another tall, blond, blue-eyed creature. By that stage, my marriage was falling apart. My husband was coming back and forth and I was getting sitters for the kids so I could go out with Ryan.

"Ryan and I were not emotionally involved. It was purely a physical thing. He came to my place freely. Again, I didn't worry about my husband being around. We went out to dinner and to movies. I wasn't afraid to be seen with him. Maybe I was ready to break out. We had a lot of sex. The sex was very different from the marriage. Sex in my marriage stunk by then. It was weird how willing Ryan was to try anything and so was I. It was a completely different experience. I found myself doing sexual things I never expected to do. I saw him four times a week. He was living with someone and I was still married but we managed to get together whenever we planned. By then I was really on my way in terms of lovers and getting free of my marriage."

Chelsea's relationship with Ryan ended because both of them had "had enough."

"We did not end on bad terms. Once he mentioned marriage, that was it for me. I'd had it and I thought he had too and then he started talking marriage. I couldn't believe it. Maybe he was in love with me, but I wasn't in love with him. No way. So I didn't see him anymore.

"The next man I met while I was married was someone I saw a few times. We went out to a restaurant and my husband learned about it. It was one of those instances where it kind of happened. First I was having drinks with this guy and then we went out. My husband took it all right, because of what he was doing with women. I continued with this guy a while longer, another short affair.

"Soon after that I met a guy, a friend of a friend, who became my lover. We met at a party and had a few drinks. I was very attracted to him. We drove in his car on the parkway and we began to do it in the car. It was a wild, strange evening. We had sex in every room, all night and through the next day. My husband wasn't around and my kids were asleep. We did it in my kids' two-foot swimming pool in the backyard and on the kitchen table. I saw this guy after that but it was never as exciting as the sex that night.

"I suppose there was no one for any length of time after Ryan, though. I would do little flings, not out of choice but because I didn't meet anyone who appealed to me beyond that. I was seeing men often but no one worth much. I stopped most of the relationships early on because I only did it for the sex and after a couple of times it was enough. I think before I was married my relationships lasted. I was engaged three other times; those were long-term. Then I had a lousy marriage so I looked for short-term, sex-driven relationships in reaction to a bad, failed marriage. When I was married and first separating and seeing other men, I was very confused about my husband. I both loved and hated him. The attraction to other men was about sex and revenge. Sometimes I did it to hurt my husband because he hurt me."

The men that Chelsea met were loosely connected through friends.

"People I knew had introduced us or I'd be at parties. The men were mostly single or divorced. Their ages were never a factor; they could be anywhere from twenty-five to fifty-five. What I'm always looking for is the blond, blue-eyed, big-shouldered, sexy man. When an affair is sex driven, it has to be about a physical attraction.

"I was never sorry, absolutely not sorry, about any affair. If anything I should have had more because you're only young once. I learned so much about sex from these different lovers. There is a right way and a wrong way to do it. I like wild, different, not kinky but rough sex. I never liked a gentle lover. I'm more the type to be thrown down on my kitchen table anytime and it's okay. Tenderness is fine on occasion, and a must at times. But from a lover, it's not what I need. I like the sex heightened and exciting. If I go to bed with a man who is no good, who is really blah, I won't see him again. I figure, why bother?

"These men have taught me things. I know that if I ever remarry, I don't plan to have lovers, but I suspect it will happen again. It certainly would if the second marriage turned out anything like the first. But if I could find a man who suited all my needs I wouldn't look elsewhere. I'm talking about someone who could be emotionally, physically and spiritually fulfilling."

Chelsea feels that once her divorce came through, she achieved an emotional rapport with her husband.

"Maybe an emotional link with my husband was only possible after the ugliness of a bad marriage was over. But we have children and so we are together on some plane. In fact, he lives in my place presently, between things, if you can believe it. Now, at last, we are friends.

"I think I looked to other men for only sex because my husband and I were lacking that the most. We suffered, then went elsewhere. With my lovers, from the start, I only wanted the sex."

The sexual issue is what drove both Chelsea's marriage and her other relationships. Her sexual satisfaction is a major concern to her. In the marriage there was one sexual relationship that didn't work and outside there were several that did not last. Basically Chelsea seems to still be in search of an emotional and physical relationship. Although she continues to operate primarily in the sexual realm, it doesn't seem to be meaningful for her.

love

affairs

3

Love Affairs

INTRODUCTION by DR. BERTRAM SLAFF

Dr. Bertram Slaff is an associate clinical professor of psychiatry at Mount Sinai Hospital and has a private practice. A past president of the American Society for Adolescent Psychiatry, he is presently the vice-president of the International Society for Adolescent Psychiatry.

Dr. Slaff began the interview by assuring me that each woman's story with her lover is unique:

"If you speak with a hundred women, there will be myriad conscious and unconscious reasons for them to take lovers. The personal needs have to be studied because the variations are enormous and one cannot generalize.

"Sexual lives are like people's fingerprints; they are individual. So while each tale is that specific, cultural attitudes are very powerful and persuasive. Whether we follow our inner lives or not is another issue. We have the ability to analyze monogamy/faithfulness as a trend of the times. For many years it was a given, an accepted way of life. Today's generation doesn't accept this unquestionably; in fact many find the concept archaic and stale.

"Thirty years ago, virginity was represented as a virtue worth preserving. Today this concept is regarded by many as foolish."

Dr. Slaff views our society as "trend driven," remarking that the sixties and seventies were actually a more liberal and free period in terms of sexual attitudes and behaviors. The AIDS crisis coincided with a moral backlash and conservative reaction. Yet one has to realize that people do continue to have affairs. Many individuals do. Do they agonize over them as they did in novels written one hundred years ago? Probably not, but often inwardly they do. Once again, it is individual.

"The question of this having a negative impact on a marriage is something one cannot take for granted. If a couple makes a decision to have affairs, then that decision has to be respected. The equilibrium with the spouse under this set of circumstances will be challenged, if there is a lover. This is a situation where things have to be worked through."

Dr. Slaff reminds us that on a biological level, there is no law that says a woman has to be married and faithful to a man for years on end.

"If one recalls Jimmy Carter, when he said that he lusted in his heart, he was ridiculed and criticized. But of course he lusted in his heart. What is a pinup girl but a model of excitement? We use *Playboy* to fantasize, which is a form of lusting in one's heart.

"People can feel guilty for their thoughts as well as for actions. I know that in the past, in rigid Catholic training, there was the belief that after the age of seven, a child was responsible for his/her thoughts. This is the opposite of psychoanalytical thinking, which accepts the ubiquity of instinctual thoughts, not subject to moralizing control. Our culture has always preached fire and damnation. Civilization imprisons people and makes rules. Without rules there is no civilization, but one begins to question them all the same. Monogamy works culturally with families, with people who have children in their structure. At best, a child is fortunate to have parents who like each other and stay together. This is the optimum situation for the child. Yet our erotic drives and our culturally-driven drives do not always remain in harmony.

"Eroticism comes from unknown factors, mostly in the subconscious. Then we work through it in terms of conscious values. For example, we can have a modern woman, feminist in terms of her beliefs, politics and the way she conducts her life. Yet she may struggle inwardly with a caveman fantasy, while believing politically that women need to be treated equally. If she is able to integrate her beliefs with her fantasies—if she can find a lover who is 'rough' but will not challenge her point of view—then it is not an irreconcilable conflict.

Dr. Slaff notes that after a period of time, a marriage can become "old shoe."

"The husband or the wife may no longer be turned on physically. It is a well-known fact that some men live out a dichotomy between the sacred and the profane. The wife is perceived as sacred, the mother of his children. From this stance, the man cannot have sex erotically with someone he respects. Since the erotic drive exists he may go elsewhere. Men, historically and socially, have always been permitted the impulse to stray, while women stayed at home and presumably accepted their plight. Today this is no longer so; women are demanding the same rights. Many women have adventures. What was formerly seen as the correct lifestyle of a community is often seen by professionals as expressive of inhibition. Those who lead such 'proper lives' are often thought to be lacking the courage to do something else, to do what they want to do."

Dr. Slaff believes that many women today do feel driven to act out their fantasies.

"If an affair fulfills the lives of some women, it still requires an amount of juggling and duplicity. In the area of consensual agreement of two people, one must take an open responsiveness to that behavior and not be quick to judge it. If an extramarital affair can provide the maximum form of self-expression with the minimal potential for destruction, we are seeing a revision of traditional values."

In Dr. Slaff's opinion, many women seek lovers not so much for sexual or erotic reasons, but because they feel a need for more attention, love and affection than their husbands are giving them. This is a common problem because so many men become addicted to their work during their middle years and have little time for or interest in their wives and domestic affairs.

Dr. Slaff recognizes the concept of women "catching up with men."

"People who have experienced romance early on in life and who have been married for enough years may begin to wonder what else is out there, what they may be missing. Women and men may have these thoughts.

"One must note that in certain marriages, an outside interest can sustain the marriage. A spouse can be very comfortable while completely aware of the arrangement. Either partner may contribute to this. It may be the wife who says to herself, So my husband is away for the weekend—why not explore?

"There is conflict between our instinctual responses and civilization's whole idea of marriage. When a young man in his twenties marries a young woman in her twenties, how can they know if it will work and what they will want in the future? They only know that they are in love at the moment and that they hope it will work out. If not, in the back of their minds there is an alternative, divorce. Or perhaps to take lovers. But when the royal family, a true symbol of society, has its own members divorcing, it becomes apparent that eventually even royalty cannot order people's emotional lives. And this brings us back to the perhaps artificial construction, that of having sex with the same person for the rest of one's life. This does not work for everyone. Some women can do it and some cannot."

The number of extramarital affairs is not what Dr. Slaff feels has changed in the last few years. "But there is a significant rise in the amount one hears about them. The culture's official point of view has changed. What is presented to us as 'the right way to be' is now being questioned in the light of women today—women who are married and take lovers."

CR&O

Eva

Originally from Philadelphia, Eva, thirty-seven, has lived on the Maryland shore her entire adult life. She was married to Charles at the age of nineteen and remained married for sixteen years. Her parents had been divorced when Eva was small, yet her orientation had been to hold on to a husband, to remain in a marriage even if it was unhappy.

She began her interview by telling us her marriage to Charles was "never any, good." And while she "loved being married," she is not sure that she ever loved Charles.

"I'm one of those people who are perfect for a monogamous relationship. Yet Charles and I didn't communicate. And we had two children right away, so there I was, married with children, financially secure and dead inside."

Several years ago, Eva met Jeff, who worked as a carpenter during the summers for Charles, building houses at the shore. Although she did not notice him for a few seasons, Eva said that after Jeff's father died, they began to communicate.

"I read in the paper that his dad had died and I felt sorry about it. We began to talk. He was poor and young, ten years younger than me, and I didn't find him attractive at first. He was the opposite of Charles, who is blond. Jeff is Italian and dark, not at all the type I go for."

Nonetheless, after a long courtship, Jeff became Eva's lover.

"By the end of that summer, I told him I thought I was in love with him. He was young and single, in college with a summer job. It took a great deal of courage on his part to return the affection. And it surprised me that he did. After Labor Day, we began to meet halfway between Philadelphia and the shore. We'd each drive forty-five minutes to sit together and talk. At first we'd just sit in his car and talk, then we went to a hotel a few times just for privacy but not for sex. And then finally we began to meet at hotels to have sex. All the love was in place by that time, so the sex was a true emotional/physical attachment. I mean he loved and adored me. It was completely different from my marriage. And the age difference was never a factor.

"I realized within a year of being married to Charles that he was absorbed with his work, even sports events on TV, but not with me. He never listened to me; he never heard what I had to say. So although we were a good team in terms of his business and socially, there was something missing. Jeff, on the other hand, listened to every word I had to say. We spent every second paying attention to each other. We got along very well. There was a real bonding and great intensity in the relationship."

Once the sex began, Eva says, "it never stopped."

"Because of the emotional attachment, the sex was so close. We waited to make love, but it was amazing, from the start. I felt more connected with Jeff, while with Charles, it was fine but it was a physical thing only. And remember, I was married so young—Jeff was the second man in my life. I'd never been around. In a sense I was very inexperienced. Although I am ten years older than Jeff, he was the one with more knowledge. The sex was much better with

Jeff than with Charles. It took longer and we did it more times a day. And it was full of love. We'd spend entire days making love. I'd say to Jeff, 'Do it 'til you're raw or not at all.' We'd both be sore but happy. Then I wouldn't see him for a few days because he'd go back to the city and I'd be with my family. But we'd be together, later in the week and we'd resume where we had left off. The sex has never changed in five and a half years. Sex is a big part of the relationship.

"One time we went to this Pocono-type hotel. We had met at a mall and it began to snow and we decided to find a hotel. Incidentally, many women meet their lovers at shopping malls. It is a place where you can easily disappear and many malls have hotels attached to them. Anyway, we ended in a place with low lights, a big bath, mirrors on the ceiling, controls on the bed, a sauna, a TV with dirty movies. It was a room for sex, definitely. And I was embarrassed when we walked in together, despite the nature of our relationship. Then we had a wild time. In this environment, you do it all. Sex, any way you imagined it. I'd say that all of our sex was like that but this hotel was hot.

"Another time we were on the Jersey Turnpike, driving along. Jeff is a very affectionate person and things got out of hand. We pulled over and did it on the turnpike, hoping a cop wouldn't come along. We had sex everywhere, on his motorcycle in the woods, and at his house we'd do it on the washing machine. It certainly was a departure from sex with Charles, lying flat in bed with the lights out."

By then Charles was conscious of the relationship and Eva told him that she was "in love."

"Charles didn't seem particularly threatened. He wasn't aware of my meetings with Jeff, and I think it came as a surprise to him when I asked for a divorce. The request was precipitated by my attraction/involvement with Jeff but in retrospect, I was trapped in a good life with something missing at the core. Today, no matter what happens, at least I know what I've shared, a wonderful relationship with Jeff, who might be the love of my life. If I hadn't had the courage to follow it through, I wouldn't have had the pleasures. As for my marriage, Jeff was the catalyst for the breakup but I should have gotten out anyway.

"At the beginning I went to a therapist because I didn't want to do anything stupid, to destroy my family and stability without understanding something about myself. The therapist encouraged me to leave once he heard what I had to say about my marriage as well as the attachment to Jeff.

"I began to understand that although my kids seemed happy because of the love and attention I gave them, they'd be happier in a situation where I was happier. And that did not necessarily mean being married to Jeff; it meant not being married to Charles. I was changing as a result of the relationship. Marriage did not seem the be-all and end-all.

"But things happened slowly. Charles and I live in a small community and we were conscious of rocking the boat. We continued to attend business and social functions together because we were worried that people would be judgmental. Charles's initial reaction to the entire episode was to try to buy me a fancy car, to entice me to stay. Meanwhile, I was totally connected to Jeff, that was where I was at. Breaking up my home was a major issue for me. The professionals I've consulted suggested it was because I came from a broken home and I'd be repeating my own history. I don't see it like that at all. I see Jeff as someone I've been lucky enough to meet and no matter what happens in the future, I've no regrets."

The divorce was difficult financially for Eva and has impacted her lifestyle.

"Although I didn't want to stay for the material comforts, I see that my girls and I have suffered because Charles tried to punish me by denying me a proper settlement. I don't miss our house or lifestyle, but a life free of financial woes is undeniably easier.

"We sold the house halfway through the divorce and I remained there until it was sold, as I'd been advised. Jeff and I have never lived together but we saw each other a few times a week throughout this ordeal. And it's fine for me that way.

"I've learned that although I'm suited for marriage, marriage might need to be redefined for me. In other words, I'm content to see Jeff on weekends and to have the space during the week to myself. The monogamy concept of marriage is fine but the day-to-day is questionable."

There has been no formal commitment from Jeff now that Eva is finally divorced, yet they continue to see one another.

"Sometimes I believe I want to be married to him for the security of it. When we first began our tryst, I wanted desperately to marry him, and to have a couple of kids immediately. But I'm not sure now. I'm worn down from the divorce and I've begun a new career in order to bring in more money. I could only sustain a weekend relationship, as I said, not full-time. I love the idea of looking forward to seeing him after the drudgery of the week. I love the excitement and happiness of getting back together. I don't need to be taken care of constantly. This way it feels like a relationship, always new and full, not a marriage. I am very happy to be alone and had I remained married to Charles, I wouldn't understand my freedom today. I've learned so much–who I am, who my friends are, who Charles really is. I listen to all my single friends, and there aren't many good men out there. They really suffer in their search. And my married friends, are they really happy?

"I've been with Jeff over five years and it's made me stronger and braver than before. It was the right thing no matter what the final outcome is. Today I recognize that having been married to Charles I should have sustained affairs from the start of our marriage, based on the kind of person he is and what my needs are. He was fine as a provider and yet we could not connect emotionally. The emotional satisfaction the right lover could offer, as well as the sexual aspect, might have proved enough supplement to keep me there. Instead I met Jeff, and he was worth my leaving. He provided me with friendship, love and sex."

Eva fits into the category of someone who uses her love affair as a vehicle to end her marriage. Yet she uses this technique in a fairly deliberate manner. She admits that from the outset of the marriage something was lacking, that emotionally there was nothing there. She stuck with the marriage for a long while because she believed it was the right thing to do, to fulfill her expectations as wife and mother.

Her romance with her lover developed in several stages. The first was not noticing Jeff, not necessarily looking for a lover. The second occurred when the idea clicked; she wanted Jeff and became obsessed with both the sex and the involvement. The third stage began when the romance took off and acquired a life of its own. Eva does not use the splitting mechanism as other women have done. She understands that her marriage did not work and that Jeff, her lover, may or may not be the answer. Grounded in tradition, she has proved independent and strong in her choice.

CRSO

Catherine

Catherine is from New Orleans, where she grew up amidst "happy WASP repression." She tells us that her childhood was "terrific" and that she was the youngest of three. Her family was an established family in the community and church life was always important to them. At the age of thirty she has been married for eight years and has two sons. This past year Catherine embarked upon an affair with a man she has known for six years.

"We met when I was twenty-four. We had an affair of the mind for years. I had actually heard of this man long before I'd ever met him. Mainly I'd heard about his wife. Women I knew had known her in college and I was anxious to meet her. We all belonged to the same church and that was how we met. Immediately my husband and I began to see my lover and his wife as a couple. They were lovely, it was social, and I was happily married. But from the beginning there was a chemistry. His wife seemed to be aware of the friendship between us. It was like a joke that never stopped, the way he flirted with me when we were all together."

Only when Catherine and her husband moved to Baton Rouge did the affair begin.

"He began to call me and invite me to lunch. It was platonic and I had a great time. But we kept it a secret from our spouses, so we knew something was going to happen. Why worry them, is the way we looked at it. We were just 'best friends.' He put me on a pedestal. He was not handsome or top-notch socially, but he wanted me and I reacted to that.

"After the sixth time, at dinner, he kissed me. It wasn't the slightest bit awkward. I remember thinking on my way home to my kids and husband, 'I'm going to have an affair.' That made life wonderful. I was always in a good mood toward my husband and my children as a result of this lover. He was a special part of my life that made me happy. There was nothing mundane about it. It was not about everyday life, children or car pools. It was about escape.

"He was definitely more interested in me than I was in him and I needed that. Gifts came in the mail. He called constantly from wherever he was. I worried if I didn't answer the phone, if I didn't get the mail. We went out to lots of nice places and I had this need to reciprocate, to pick up the check every other time so I didn't feel like a prostitute. I didn't want to be beholden.

"And then I got competitive. I wanted to look better than his spouse. The whole time she was my friend and I kept thinking she was the better person. I felt, strangely enough, fine about my spouse throughout all this, not one bit torn. I never felt guilty about him. I never had trouble sleeping with two men at once.

"It was after that first kiss that I knew we were going to have sex. And sure enough it began. He would travel to see me, sometimes four times a week. By then we were having sex all the time. I have a high sexual drive and he did not respond as my husband would. He certainly was not as good as my husband, but the foreplay with someone else is so much more exciting. It doesn't matter if he's a better lover—it's just that he is excited and that made me excited. He was not as expert or as familiar as my husband so not as good technically, but I was very turned on to the experience."

Catherine's lover sent her notes and poems continually.

"His notes to me were all about how in the eyes of God there couldn't be a purer love. He wrote about how hard it was at times not to be with me. He never mentioned his wife or my husband in these letters. I was worried, worried about how fast the whole relationship was moving. Yet neither of us wanted to leave our spouses. Both of us cared too much for family and lifestyle to leave. We understood it was a true affair in every sense, from the start. He always said his mistake was that he 'fucked with his heart.'"

When asked if she felt as if she was leading two lives at once, Catherine replied that she most definitely did.

"I'd always been organized with my life but this was a lot of juggling for me. The business of meeting for sex and arranging my children's schedule was demanding. I realize now that I fulfilled a sexual fantasy for him, although we were positively in love with each other. The sexual intimacy was the least of it for me. I'm a very modest person and I remained so during the affair. We were involved in every way. He came on to me. I liked him initially because he liked me. He'd always told me how special I was. I returned the affection. My husband is not a demonstrative person and he never tells me that he loves me. I was partly angry at him. I was angry because he never gives me attention and because he never gives me money. It was everything together. What I wished was that my husband would be the one to support me, emotionally and financially. Then I might not have gone with my lover.

"But I did. He said things that made me feel good. The sex with my lover was not so important although I lied and told him it was. It wasn't as much fun as being with him, as doing things with him. We had sex in our river house, right on our property. Always we did it during the day, which fit into my schedule. In the summer we'd meet for early dinners."

Catherine describes herself as "so happy" while the affair lasted.

"For eight months I was ecstatic. Then his wife found out that he was seeing someone. She accused him and it began to fall apart. He got worried and frightened. I was worried sick for myself. I worried that she suspected me. It never occurred to me that he'd leave me at the threat of discovery. I was shocked and amazed when it happened. Often we had discussed it and he said on occasion that he'd leave his wife. I never believed that; I think it was said only in a fit of passion. But I didn't think the reverse was true, that he'd simply go away.

"I was very disappointed and hurt. I would have kept on with it. It was so intense, that was the problem. I knew it had to end because of the pace. But I never expected it to happen so soon, so abruptly. Once he wanted to end it, I felt totally betrayed and that nothing he'd ever said was the truth. Then maybe we both spoke out of both sides of our mouths in the midst of things. I'd wait by the phone all day long after the upset. He would still call but not three or four times a day. I was obsessed with him, still."

Catherine explains the nature of the relationship as all-consuming from start to finish.

"I was totally absorbed in it. I would only wear black because he loved me in it. I went and bought all these black outfits. Somehow, somewhere, during the height of the affair, when we met and made love, I understood—we had to try to transfer the shared joy to our marriages. I wanted us to try to take it toward what lacked in the marriages. But that was unrealistic, I suppose, and confusing. Maybe it came out of guilt. I think that having been raised in the South my whole approach to a man is to please him. My husband has been the recipient of my energy but my lover was the giver. That was refreshing; it did good things for me personally. I got thin, I concentrated on my clothes. Of course I ignored my friends and I lied to people in order to see him. I never had to lie to my husband because he was never around. I never told anyone about this affair."

Today Catherine understands why women have affairs.

"It was an awakening, sexually and emotionally. I had another life. A side of myself I'd never seen before came out. I became territorial, jealous of his wife, his time. And then the begging. I'm ashamed that I begged him to continue. I guess I wanted the upper hand. I wonder how other women feel about the pain it evokes. I experienced pain beyond pain. It was like an old Japanese poem about a limb being cut off. Today, so soon afterwards, I'm missing not only my lover but a best friend who I spoke to constantly. So I lost two things at once, a friend and a lover. I feel my arm has been amputated but the pain continues. I remind myself that my lover told me that he loved me too much, that he couldn't handle the balance. Isn't that bullshit if he's gone? How could he so abruptly end it?"

Catherine has returned to her husband, "emotionally" on some level.

"I don't trust my lover anymore and I will always trust my husband. From making my ego strong, my lover devastated me. I cannot say that I embrace my marriage in response to this disappointment, but I certainly have gone home to it on some level. I think about how I never lied to my lover and how I cannot accept what he's done to me. On the other hand, I'm beginning to recover and to feel stronger every day. It goes in waves. I listen to songs on the radio and everything seems to fit my story. Finally, I have little regret. I did it for me and I'm only sorry it ended."

The story Catherine tells us is very complex. Because she atypically initiated the affair, characterizing it as "an affair of the mind," it is evident that she had different expectations than most women. What developed into a love affair ended up devastating her in the end.

Her lover's withdrawal of love is extremely painful to her. Ultimately it was not particularly satisfying sexually or emotionally. The sex was minimal so that she experienced little guilt in sleeping with two men at once. She was quite hurt by the abruptness of the finish. It was not what she expected. It seems she really suffered when he terminated the affair.

ⓒ੩୫ଠ

Marilyn

Marilyn comes from southern California, where she presently lives. Twenty years into her marriage she began a romance with a lover. At the age of fifty-two, she believes that until she began this other relationship she was very happy and that the marriage and raising four children were a successful endeavor.

"After so many years, not only did I get involved with someone, but he was my brother-in-law, my husband's brother. I know it sounds sticky and ridiculous, but I had always been attracted to him, for years. We had a business dealing together. He told me to stop by his office and one thing led to another. By then his marriage was almost over but mine was not. In fact, I never had any intention of leaving my marriage for him. And my husband never found out about the affair.

"I think perhaps that while I loved my husband, I was always in love with his brother. It lasted for four years, and during that time I was absolutely thrilled to be with my lover."

By the time the affair began, Marilyn's lover was separated and his apartment was available.

"Mostly we'd go to his apartment but we also use people's beach houses that were empty off-season, and ski houses. I'd see him two or three times a week. I found my lover listened to what I had to say, and when we met each other there was a lot of talking as well as a lot of sex. My lover was in love with me and I always knew that, which helped. In a way, because he was my brother-in-law, it was easier to see him. I'd see him at family social gatherings and it was fine. I'd say to myself, at least I'm seeing him, even if the terms were not what I chose.

"I felt very guilty for a long time. I had one confidante, one friend who would listen to me. It was the brother-in-law aspect of the affair that made me feel so guilty. Then I became ambivalent about my husband while it was going on. I'd look at him and hope he'd listen to me but he was the same. I was the one who was changing. His brother listened to what I had to say."

The sex, Marilyn feels, was "terrific" and far superior to the sex she had with her husband.

"The sex was great, really remarkable. We had sex all the time. I sometimes found myself sleeping with both men on the same night. It seemed like a joke to me. It was exciting and interesting. I admit it seemed to add a spark to my life. I became more vain, more concerned with how I looked. While I was always that way, it was more so. And often I'd think how much better looking my husband was than his brother but it didn't matter; I felt as I felt."

Ultimately, Marilyn believes that her marriage and children never suffered as a result of the affair.

"I could see that I was able to keep it a separate part of my life. I never mixed the two and, therefore, I was a mother and a wife. I was simply a lover too. I was able to pay attention to everyone who needed me. I could handle that. I never intended to leave my husband as a result of the affair. I thought that leaving him for another was simply trading new problems and new bullshit for the old. It never seemed worth it to me. I'm certainly not sorry that I did it, though. For everywhere we were together, hotels, restaurants, movies, every public place, whether we really should have or not, it was so nice to be with him. I wanted to be with him, that was the thing. That's why I'm not sorry at all. Because we did not live in the same town, we would drive places to meet one another. We drove long distances to meet sometimes, so we weren't always cavalier about being seen. But if we felt it was comfortable to be seen and acceptable under the circumstances, we went ahead. So our meeting places varied but it was a constant thing to meet. We met regularly no matter what it required to get there."

Eventually the affair "died down" due to a series of events.

"I suppose that as it came it went. But I also think that his divorce coming through had something to do with it. My husband died and that broke it off. Before that, though, my lover wanted to date and see other women. I began to realize it would never be me, no matter what I'd understood all along. That was the bottom line, hope against hope.

"It was a true affair, an isolated incident. I never wanted others even as I saw him begin to date. I knew it wasn't going to work. For the time it had existed as an emotional/physical obsession. That phased out and the intensity was diluted. I don't believe that these things can ever sustain that kind of intensity anyway. I felt the affair had no bearing on the rest of my life until my life changed. Then it had to be examined and reevaluated. Today my lover is remarried and so am I. Everyone is happy and I have no regrets."

Marilyn's situation is complicated, in large part owing to family connections. Choosing her husband's brother as her lover might reflect some hostility toward her husband. Yet the caring for her husband did not wane. The feelings for her lover were something different.

Marilyn was capable of sustaining both relationships for a long period of time. In the end, it yielded to circumstance, and life events controlled the outcome.

CB80

Christine

Christine's childhood and adulthood in Albany were described by her as "very elite and very sheltered." Having gone directly from college to marriage with a "father figure," she seems to have always sustained a superficial happiness. Even when she discusses her relationship with her lover, she describes it as if it exists without anger or stress.

In her late thirties, Christine has been married for over fifteen years. Yet her marriage overwhelmed her from the start.

"My husband is a number of years older and we had four children in rapid succession. My husband is a workaholic and runs a large business. He is rarely at home. Perhaps because I don't work and I have babysitting help, I was faced with an odd combination of time on my hands and so many children who needed me as much as possible. At any rate, I felt overloaded."

Christine met her lover at a small seaside community which she and the children move to every summer. Her husband only visited on certain weekends, so she found it an "easy scenario to pull off."

"When we first began to go to the beach, I was startled by the simplicity of it. And then I met someone, someone who made it the most amazing place to spend my time, someone who changed my life once and for all. I met a man my age, unmarried, who was spending his summer at the beach, studying for the bar examination. We ran into each other at a few parties and after a while we'd meet on the beach at the end of the day to talk.

"Within weeks we became lovers. There we were in a small beach town where everyone knew everyone, not like a city which affords anonymity. In fact my in-laws knew his parents. It was so interwoven, but that had little impact on us. We were determined to carry out our affair."

Christine invited her lover to her home late at night or they met on the dunes to have "wild unending sex."

"Our affair began in 1990 and is still going strong. My lover has never married and he plans his entire life around the times that I can see him. Unbelievable as it seems, I have been pulling this off for over eleven years and I feel the same about my lover and about my husband as I did the day it began. They say you can only love one person at a time, but I seem to love two. I adore my husband– he treats me with respect, buys me what I want and is very supportive. But my lover is very special as well. He seems to have more time for me, something I'm not able to get from my husband because most of his time is devoted to his business or to the children's athletic activities. My lover is cultured and erudite; I never tire of listening to him. And the sex is always a part of it. The sex is special too."

The relationship, including vacations, has followed the same routine for all this time. That is, typically she will meet her lover for lunch one day a week unless her husband is traveling, and then she will meet him more often. Afterward she'll go shopping with her friends until her lover leaves work, and they spend the evening together. At eleven o'clock she returns home. Her husband believes that Christine is shopping downtown with friends.

"All of my friends know about the relationship and would protect me to the bitter end. But the vacations work the best. Whenever and wherever we vacation, my lover goes to the same spot. I am able to see him there. If it is a ski vacation, I simply tell my husband that I'm too tired one or two days and then I meet my lover. My family suspects nothing. Summers still remain the easiest situation for us, though, because my lover is always at the place where he now owns a summer home, where we first met. And in sentimental terms it is our spot. My lover takes off a chunk of time and spends it at the beach with me."

Recently Christine's lover has begun to make demands on her, and she is waiting to see the outcome.

"After many years of sustaining two love affairs, one a marriage with children and one a kind of marriage, without children, and with less flexibility, my lover is complaining. He's getting older now and wants to settle down, and have a family. He wants me to leave my husband and marry him, have children with him, but I would never dissolve my marriage. I couldn't do that to my husband and to my children. Besides, it is a matter of lifestyle. While my husband certainly provides me with every comfort, my lover could do the same. Yet I already have children with my husband and they are growing up and I'm glad of that. Since my lover is my age and not older, he is ready to begin a family. This is no longer an interest of mine. My choice would be to simply continue as is. For the time being, I want both my lover and husband in my life. Having two relationships all these years has been enjoyable. What one man can't satisfy, the other man can."

One could speculate that there might be more to Christine's story. Perhaps her husband is aware of this long-standing affair and has his own reasons to leave things as they are. It appears that Christine does not need to work especially hard to keep both relationships functioning. The question, then is—on what level of seriousness do they operate? If both her marriage and her affair are low-expectation matters, then success is easier to achieve. As with any relationship—with its demands and tugs, the pulls and stresses of everyday life—the less superficial it is, the more difficult it is to keep in play. Thus we question the texture and depth of Christine's relationship with her lover.

The absence of guilt is striking. Such long-term duplicity is difficult for many women to sustain. The constancy of two relationships of this duration becomes too demanding. However, Christine is able to handle both; she takes from each man what is offered. Perhaps because her needs are answered in this way she is satisfied, and free of guilt.

ᏟᎦᎬᏅ

Joanna

Joanna is thirty-nine years old and lives on Long Island. She has three children; two are stepchildren and one is her own. Married at twenty-four for the first time, the marriage lasted four years. Her second marriage is the one that produced a child, and lasted eight years. For the duration of both marriages, and the time in between, Joanna has conducted an affair with the same man.

Describing her childhood, Joanna tells us that her father was "absent" by the time she was thirteen, having remarried a "jealous woman" who "basically took him away." She believes her parents' divorce and her father's "abandonment" greatly affected her life. Today Joanna lives with two of her children and is in the process of being divorced. Categorizing her story as an "epic," Joanna began with her first husband.

"My first marriage was to a slightly reluctant bachelor who didn't really want to marry me. He was in the television business and traveled a lot. We had no children and I often felt as if I was single. I had a relationship with another man from the start of my marriage to the end. The other man, Michael, was someone I'd known for two years before I was married. I was in graduate school and I met him on a summer job. He was a few years older and I was very young, very attracted to him. But I had a boyfriend and I was into seeing many people, footloose and fancy-free. I was, as I remember, young and wild.

"I lied to him about my summer job and he thought I was there for good. So when I left in the fall to go back to school, he was surprised. He had a wife who was pregnant and had never cheated before. He was really a one-person-at-a-time kind of guy. That year I fell in love with him. It became an intense affair once I no longer saw him daily. I was back at school and we called each other every day. We saw each other once a week."

Joanna explains the sex as "immediate" and a major part of the relationship.

"I seduced him right off the bat. The sex was not great the first time and then it was fabulous. I was very cityish and he was very suburban and married, nervous and reluctant. I'd say, 'C'mon, what the hell?' because his being married didn't bother me a bit at that point. I didn't give a shit. I knew that he saw me as different and exciting. I'd sneak my mother's car and drive anywhere to be with him. We went to great lengths to be together. Mostly we had sex in the city at hotels. We also used his cousin's apartment and his friend's apartment, on Central Park West.

"Michael didn't know many people in the city so he felt safe there. He didn't like clubs or late nights so mostly we met to eat and have sex. He was happy but confused and he definitely felt guilty. I didn't care that he had a family. He was important to me in the beginning as a very good friend. We talked a lot, everywhere, in bed, on the phone."

Michael, although married, did not like it when Joanna had boyfriends and was quite affected by her marriage.

"Finally, after two years, I got married because I wanted a life of my own. Michael said he'd never leave his wife and while I didn't have the same communication with my husband, I knew I had to try. My lover, Michael, and I never stopped seeing each other. I showed him the proofs of my wedding, I remember that. We sort of cooled it for a while but we still met and talked. I missed the rest of the relationship. My first husband traveled often and the first year I traveled with him some although I was working full time. By the second year the marriage seemed impossible. He was not a good husband so I didn't go with him on any of his trips. The whole time I saw Michael as much as I could. I felt practically single and I was with my lover three times a week, at least. Mostly we were at my apartment because my husband was away so much. But I remember we went to Boston together."

At that time, Joanna had a miscarriage and wondered if the child was her lover's or her husband's.

"Probably this baby was Michael's because my husband was away so much. I was so sick and bleeding so much and my husband never came home when I was in the hospital. When he did get back, I told him it was over. By then Michael had two children and I was very pissed off about the second kid. I wanted him to leave his wife–I'd gotten to that stage. Meanwhile, he didn't want me to leave my husband, because while I was married it was safe."

At that point, Joanna met her second lover.

"When I was separating I met a young guy, five years younger, drop-dead gorgeous, the cover of *GQ* gorgeous. I was someone else's wife but I began to see him. He was the most adorable, most fun guy. We went to Fire Island on his boat, to clubs, all fun places. He practically moved in with me. I said to my steady lover, I'm free now and I can see whoever I want. However, I will never see another man as long as I live if you will leave your wife for me. Michael refused and I stopped seeing him."

With the young lover Joanna had "incredible sex" and she spent the summer with him, avoiding her steady lover, Michael.

"The young guy was a real hunk, Hollywood hunky, but also he was such a sweet person. The attraction was physical, though; he was everything my other lover wasn't physically. Also, he was free and easy. We could stay out all night, so I guess his style was the opposite of Michael's too. He had this gorgeous body and was very sexual. We had lots of sex. It drove my lover crazy. This lover was out of a Calvin Klein ad.

"Although I stopped seeing Michael, one night when we were out we ran into each other. I was with the young guy, who said to Michael, 'I hope you make her happy because she's crazy about you.' It was a hot summer romance and I was sort of sad when it ended. We mutually broke off because Michael said he was going to leave his wife and the young lover thought that he was still going back to school. In other words, by autumn, he no longer wanted to party. But right before it ended, one thing happened. I lied to Michael about my plans in order see this guy. Michael followed us and he came up to my apartment and the young lover hid. He screamed at me, 'You fucking liar,' and then he left. I was frantic because I realized he was the one I loved. It was the last straw for the other romance. I knew I wanted Michael. Soon after that, I was divorced.

"Sometimes I think if I hadn't had a crummy husband I might have stayed married. Michael and I were liars. We lied to each other, we lied to our spouses. I had no faith we'd ever get together but I left my marriage anyway. We went to L.A. together for a week and after that he was in love with me. He moved into a hotel but he was depressed and guilt-ridden. Then, despite therapy, he changed his mind again and went back to her. I was heartbroken. He said he felt guilty, that we'd done something terrible. He bought me jewels and chased me but he pretended it was all my fault. We needed to work out the boundaries, but he couldn't leave his wife."

It was then that Joanna married a man with two young children.

"He was a widower, several years younger than me. I was never in love with him but I was in love with what he stood for—stability, family. I told him about my lover. That was probably the first mistake. The marriage lasted eight years. For the first year of the marriage, I didn't see Michael. I missed him terribly. Then we got going again. He and I met in the parking lot where we'd always met. He said he missed me and loved me. I told him if he wanted me and wanted to start up again, we needed an apartment together. And furnished nicely. We needed a love nest. I wouldn't go to hotels anymore; I was beyond that business of sneaking around. A part of me wasn't even sure about Michael at that stage. I had managed without the affair being so intense a part of my life."

When asked about Michael's marriage, Joanna replies that she did not focus on it. She wanted a baby and didn't want to leave her new marriage. She decided to stop demanding that Michael leave his.

"I was still working and then I was taking care of my husband's children. But I wanted a baby of my own. I was determined after having miscarried and having had two abortions to have my own child. I loved and adored my stepchildren, who were like my own, but I wanted to be pregnant. I really began to feel, when I returned to Michael then, that I was living a life within a life.

"Two years into the marriage and the resumed affair, I got pregnant. Michael questioned if the baby was his. This time it wasn't. I told him I'd been so careful with my diaphragm, which seemed to trouble him. I told him I'd given up my whole life for him and that I wanted my husband's baby. I said if he wanted a baby with me, to do it the right way, to leave his wife. His own marriage was falling apart and I heard his wife was having an affair. Then I heard that Michael and his wife had gone on a nice vacation. That set me off and I went into premature labor.

"Something snapped once my child was born, and my lover and I became more blatant about being together, less careful. We went away together with the baby. I took help along so we were together constantly, having great sex. We had this apartment we shared and we used beepers to leave messages for each other. We were never where we were supposed to be in order to lead our double life. During the weekends Michael was Mr. Suburban and during the week he was my lover. I'd talk to him on the phone nightly, pretending he was a girlfriend. Every spring we went away together, and I would tell my husband that I was visiting a girlfriend. My friend was my alibi. My husband was unhappy that I didn't sleep with him much and was half hoping it wasn't the truth, half naive. I felt the most guilt about leaving the kids at night, saying I was going to the gym. I'd lie all the time; the lies were terrible. I became angrier and angrier at my husband, who had lost his money and was moving me further away from my sister and friends, as we had to sell house after house. I was so far from the apartment that Michael and I kept, it was difficult.

"We met every Saturday morning. Whenever we were together we made love and ate. He loves restaurants and so do I. He always wanted to be out in public, which worried me. I noticed we didn't go out to restaurants where he lived, but he didn't mind doing it where I lived. It made me nervous. What finally happened was that we went to Florida together and as he was passionately kissing me, I looked up and saw my neighbor. This woman told everyone. I lost three friends. Even a friend who was having an affair told me I was wrong. My husband didn't hear, which surprised me. Then we moved again and I tried once more to be a mother and wife, but the love affair never died down. It was the same passion. We always yearned for each other."

Several months ago, Joanna's lover left his wife and Joanna decided to stay with her husband because he was in a bad financial situation.

"I told him I no longer wanted to live with him as if we were married but I'd stay until he was able to straighten things out. I got to know Michael's children and I've stayed in touch with my stepchildren. But when I look back on my life, I see that I gave Michael the best years, because this is the love of my life. I've had two marriages; I have no husband, no money and no financial security. And I'm only interested in living with Michael and having him buy a house, which he'll put in my name. He very much wants to get married and we talk about a baby. Some days I want his baby, and other days I think I'm past the stage of having one, on to other things."

Joanna is relieved that she no longer has to "lie and sneak."

"For every year we had to lie, I'll be happy for five that we no longer lie. It still feels like a love affair. Michael's afraid that until we live together, when he moves in next week, it will be a love affair. But I say we had to go forward, no more dating. It sucks, the meetings, the stolen time. I'm turning forty and if he doesn't meet my deadlines, to live together, it will be too late. Either we move forward together or good-bye."

Joanna's story is very poignant. She was confused initially about how to develop a relationship with a man so that it became a partnership. She explored other men because of the unavailability of her lover. Although she never articulates this, there might be a part of her that was fearful of committing to a man in a complete way. However, this seems to be a true love story.

CR80

Robin

Robin comes from a small town in the Northeast and lives there presently with her husband and three children. Her childhood was a "very normal, very happy" one. Her parents' marriage was intact and she was a "good girl who pleased them." Married at twenty-four, she has been married for seventeen years.

"My marriage was really fine until I met this man. I met him at a shopping center in our hometown. He was one of those men who women notice immediately, a true womanizer. He gave me a look and I felt he was looking through me. He was someone who has had many affairs while I was someone who had experienced none.

"He seemed to like me but I was so naive. I had no idea what it was about. We became friendly and after four weeks we ended up in bed. After six months of seeing him, I no longer felt guilty. In fact, I believe that a woman who has an extramarital relationship becomes so involved with her lover that the guilt disappears. That was what happened to me."

Robin was thirty-two years old when the attachment began and it has been going on for the last eight years. Her lover is also married and has two children.

"I knew from the start I'd gotten myself into a real mess but I went forward anyway. I was in a vulnerable state when we met, having just stopped work to mother three small children full-time. My husband has always been a workaholic and that contributed to my feeling of being adrift and alone. This man has such flexible hours–he could be with me often, at any time of day. I needed the attention and I wanted his companionship.

"During the summers we were together practically every day. I did absolutely outrageous things in order to be with him. We introduced our spouses and children to each other and became family friends, orchestrating family vacations and Sundays together. My lover became like a second father to my kids. It was ironic because he is in a bad marriage and doesn't love his wife and seems less connected to his own kids than to mine. Meanwhile my husband is someone I do love. And he can't be with the kids a lot because of work, but he is devoted to our family. So our situations were not exactly the same. Always I was aware of my love for my children and my commitment to them. The relationship never interfered with my kid's needs. It was a separate life."

The family get-togethers were "relaxed and cool," according to Robin, and she "had no trouble" with the fact that her lover and her husband were friendly. This setup worked for the first four years and only became "hellish" three or four years ago, when Robin wanted to end the affair.

"After four years, I'd had it. But my lover told me that he'd tell my husband if I left him. He was blackmailing me and I loved him enough to let him do it. I was trapped by then, really trapped. The concept of loving two men at once was never a problem for me, but getting caught at it was something else. I was very concerned about it."

Eventually Robin's situation moved into another phase when she insisted several months ago that her lover leave her and find someone else.

"As emotionally and physically linked as I was and as I am, I simply couldn't take the deceit anymore. I know that after so many years, one wonders why it suddenly began to bother me, but it did. I realize that he's a cheat and is not a good person. My husband is a better person. He's also more successful and more handsome. And still I can't really leave this other man.

"I told him to go but I didn't mean it because I didn't want him to actually do it. Not in my heart. Then I struggled with this thought that I needed a normal life, that I couldn't go on like this, that it was sick."

Robin feels that the relationship was "never driven by sex." Yet she describes the sex with her lover as "better than in the movies."

"While sex with my husband has always been fine, it was not great. With my lover, it's so incredible it's hard to give up. I'd like to make love to him for the rest of my life. It began in a calm manner. I was cautious, a most afraid. After all, I hadn't slept with someone else in ten years. Then the sex became wild and crazy. We did it every way possible, we invented things. We went beyond expectations, beyond anything I ever dreamed of.

"I never slept with both men the same day. I was lucky; I was able to control when I had sex with my husband. And I never did the same things with my husband sexually. He wouldn't ask me to, because he knew I would refuse. But I did them with this man, gladly."

According to Robin, the positive aspects of her connection to another man included her family. She believes that both she and her lover were better to their spouses and their children when they were happy with each other.

"We even opened a company together, as a front. We wanted to be business partners, to have that time together. In the beginning it was fine for both our marriages."

Today Robin's life is in turmoil and she doubts what her own needs are.

"I love him and I love my husband. I don't think that my husband has any idea what has gone on. I don't know what I want anymore. I sent him away. I was cruel and insensitive because I wanted a life without complications, but I realize that if he does go I won't be okay. I mean we wanted to marry each other while we were married to our spouses—we were that involved. We wanted to have a marriage without leaving our spouses, to unite us. That was when I thought things were in balance, that I had a husband who got what he wanted from me and a lover who had what he wanted. Now that's all changed. My lover has found a girlfriend and I don't think I can wait for him to return to me. For so long he was devoted and the idea that I rejected him hurts me. I'm very confused."

Robin continues to see her lover while she struggles with her plans for the future.

"This is a passion. I look at this guy and I die. Now that he's found a younger woman, I ask myself, Do I let him go, or share him, or do I wait? I feel so responsible. I still want him. I think I want to marry him, but I don't want to give up my life as it is. Then I think I can't go back to the way it was… I want to marry him in order to move forward. I'm beyond the scandal of our town and friends. If he isn't there for me, if it's too late, I'm not sure what I'd do. That's where I am today, struggling with the choices that wait for me. Presently I am with my marriage and with my lover."

Robin's relationship with her lover is an overwhelming attachment. Her whole life has been organized around the structure of being with this man. She is committed at a level beyond her control.

She is aware on some level of the obsessive aspect of her relationship, but is unable to change the setup at present. The final story is not yet out, and what will happen remains to be seen.

CRED

Samantha

Samantha, at the age of twenty-nine, has three young children and is married for the second time. She lives in an "average town" in Nebraska, where she was raised. Her family was middle class, and her parents were divorced before she was born. By the time Samantha was two, her mother had remarried a man she describes as verbally abusive. Her childhood was "terrible," based on her relationship with her stepfather.

"My stepfather ruined my childhood. I bring him up because I think it had bearing on how I conducted my early adult life. I was disowned by my stepfather when my mother died of cancer. That happened during my first year of college. I learned that my real father was also dead by then, a man I'd never met. I did not feel good about men at that time. I'd always had boyfriends for long periods of time in high school. I think I needed the stability there that I never had at home. My mother was powerless. My boyfriends came from nice families and I got taken under their wing.

"When I was in my last year of college I broke up with a long-standing boyfriend because I'd met a guy in a band. I lived with him and I kind of pushed him toward getting married. This marriage lasted over four years. When we were married for a few weeks, he was already running around. Of course, I didn't know at the time. Basically, when I did learn about it, I was angry. We were both very young. We had a house, though, and we made good money, both of us. We seemed an ideal couple to everyone else. But I knew that he kept rolling in at four in the morning. He denied it every time I asked if he saw other women. He said it was the band, his work with the band that kept him out so late."

Samantha thought her husband was "unemotional and cold." She began to see that he was similar to her stepfather.

"I realized too late that he reminded me of my stepfather, that I'd had some need to do that, to relive that. He would never kiss me, my husband. We had sex, but really I was there to be the wife. The sex was fine but short. Nothing that rocked the walls. I knew by then that he was with other women, despite his denials. Every weekend he played in the band by night and during the week he worked a nine-to-five job. I used to go to the clubs with him, to see him perform, but he began to tell me not to come. Then I wanted something for me besides my job. I am a technician. I got involved in theater and I realized I could sing and dance. I found all the satisfaction I never found in my life. There were people all around; there was a connection. All that was missing from home was right there.

"One day I went to an audition and read opposite an actor. The director liked us together. While the show ran, we became good friends. We spent a lot of time together. He was several years younger, and I was married, but we began to date. It became something. At first we'd go out in groups and then we began to go back to his apartment. This happened after a few months of working together."

When Samantha and her lover became involved, she thought she was drawn to him because he was unlike her husband.

"He was a great guy, everything my husband wasn't. He was sweet and kind and considerate. He was very young but very mature. He worked computers and held a full-time job as I did. We both loved theater and that was a common bond.

"The sex was amazing. The first time, he moved the earth. There I was, with this younger guy who knew I was married, and I only felt guilty about getting caught. Deep down I must have felt the guilt. The only concern I had was immediate, that I get home by three because my husband would be out until five. I really liked this guy by then; I was most definitely involved with him. I'd wanted to sleep with him for a long time before it happened. He was so caring. It's incredible how very different two men can be. Entirely different creatures. It shows in everything, even in the sex. My lover and I had this mutual worship.

"I learned so much about sex from him. He was not more experienced, but we were so drawn to each other, we did it like rabbits. We would make love for hours on end. It never stopped, this intense—wildly intense—sex."

By then Samantha was seeing her lover as often as possible, believing that her husband did not know or care.

"We got together four or five times a week. My husband was so preoccupied with other facets of his life he never noticed. I no longer loved him in the least and I wanted to get out of the marriage and marry my lover. My lover was so young and he was scared to death.

There I was, an older married woman. He had to think about it for a long while, which was a torture to me. Then he came to me and made a serious commitment.

"I think he knew how deep our attraction went. He was attractive to me as a person, every bit of who he was. I thought he was much handsomer than my husband, something I might not have thought at first. I was so totally uninvolved with my husband by then and so involved with my lover. I alienated myself from my husband and he didn't seem concerned. I didn't want to sleep with him anymore once I was with my lover. That was difficult because, I was afraid he'd pick up on that. I sort of balanced both at the start.

"Everyone was from the same town, which was weird. My lover's family was of another order; his dad was a professional. Just the fact that we were all there in the same place made it seem more on the edge. For a while I was leading two lives and I knew I had to move on. I had to make a decision. I had material things for the rest of my life, a house, two cars, but the marriage was nothing. My lover had nothing material but he was who I wanted to be with. After eight months of the affair, I decided to leave the marriage."

Samantha's husband was astonished when she requested a separation.

"My husband couldn't believe me. He swore he had had no affairs, ever. After taking the marriage for granted, he realized he loved me. He begged, he followed, he spied on us. He had a confrontation with my lover. He told him to leave me alone, not to steal his wife. He swore his innocence and told everyone that I was the vixen. He played a very heavy mind game on me. He eventually came back and told me he had indeed slept with other women all during the marriage. I knew it. I think deep down inside you know when something like that is happening to you. I definitely had sensed it when it was going on. And maybe my husband had sensed it with me."

At the start of the marriage Samantha had wanted a baby very much. Once she was no longer with her husband sexually, she decided to wait.

"After I'd kept trying to have a baby, I saw a doctor who told me I'd have great difficulty conceiving. I sort of let it go and then while I was separated I got pregnant. My husband found out and immediately filed for divorce because he didn't want to pay for the baby. I guess he panicked. That was when he drew the line and stopped any communication with me. I knew it was my lover's baby. I expected my lover to panic over the situation. He did the opposite. Our friends were mortified at the whole story. I was determined to have a child on my own, no matter what my lover chose to do, or what anyone said. I wouldn't marry him until after the baby was born. I didn't want to be one of those brides who have to do it. When I gave birth, we decided to get married."

Married to her lover, with small children, Samantha describes her life as "wonderful."

"I am blissfully happy. Had I not met this man, I believe I would have stayed in the marriage. I would have kept trying to have a baby with my husband to avoid the other part of the relationship. I think I also would have stayed with him because it avoided the broken home I came from. Giving up material comforts and leaving a marriage was a big decision for me. But I knew it was worth the risk; my lover had shown me that.

"I trust my present husband completely and that is very unlike the first marriage. Not in a million years would I bat an eye when he goes out alone. I have total faith. I think about the differences in each marriage. At my first wedding, my husband decided to take his wedding band off before the reception. When I eloped with my lover, he told me he couldn't wait to wear his wedding ring. That about sums it up. I know now that I broke away from my own family environment completely when I left the first marriage. I finally broke free."

Samantha's story is compelling. This is a woman who sort of slid into a marriage to repair the damage done to her in her childhood. It was an attempt to put things right because of the tragic, traumatic nature of the loss of her mother and the relationship with her stepfather.

What happened was that her plan backfired and her husband was not who she expected him to be. With the lover, it was the same motivation to repair the damage. In this situation she was either more fortunate or more astute, and it worked out successfully.

CRED

Nicole

Nicole describes her childhood as "terrific." An only child from a town in the South, she attended a girls' school and then a women's college for two years. Always she was attracted to men. While she claims her experience was limited, e.g., she was unfamiliar with minorities until her parents moved to New York, she had her eyes wide open to any excitement that might come her way. She told us that once she'd transferred to a university she dated "everything that wore pants: professors, townies, students, frat boys, law students, premed, business students—sometimes three and four men a day. One for breakfast, one for lunch and one for dinner. The last date was late evening. I had a ladder and climbed out of my dorm or someone climbed in."

Thus Nicole's conventional upbringing was challenged when she was at an impressionable age by her exposure to a variety of people, particularly men.

"I only slept with some. If they were marriageable I wouldn't sleep with them, and by the time I was twenty-three, I was married to a picture-perfect man. He was a preppie, WASP with blue eyes and handsome. We had a picture-perfect wedding and remained married for thirteen years."

During this time, Nicole had a long-standing affair with a man who later became her second husband. It began in the tenth year of her marriage. They were introduced at work. Both she and her lover were married at the time. She perceives herself as "a woman men pay a lot of attention to," and her relationship with the other partner was not really a surprise to her. When asked if she loved them both, she said perhaps she did, or perhaps she loved neither one.

"I thought I was in love with them both when it was happening, but I was in the middle of it, so who can judge? The relationship was sexual. It was all about sex. Sex like I'd never known before, total abandon; no part of my body seemed uninteresting. In fact, it was all extremely interesting to him. Nor was any part of my body unworthy of exploration. I'd blink and hours would be gone. That was how it seemed when we were together. I mean my eyeballs would roll. There, are few men who can stay with that kind of thing, that kind of sex. I believe it's an unusual man who puts a woman ahead of himself in bed. Someone who takes himself less seriously. He'd put his tongue around my ankle and bring my whole body alive. It was very tactile.

"Robert was several years younger, and now I know age doesn't mean anything. It's how they relate to me, these men. It's not age, looks or position. It's not religion, money; it's only how they handle the moment. Do they dwell on the past or focus on the future? Are they able to enjoy the present? Can they live for the day? To be intimate with me, the person has to live the day. That was Robert's charm in the beginning. Because we only had the day, stolen moments. It was fabulous and exciting.

"The first time we spent the night together was in the city, at a hotel. We were both there on business, at dinner. Later on I was having trouble with the key to my door, you know the ones you push in like a credit card, and I ended up with him. The sexual energy had been flowing all night. Then I couldn't do it again, spend the night with Robert. I had a husband and child in the suburbs. So we'd sneak time together, often, whenever, wherever we could. He was on an expense account...we did the town. My only concern was that James, my husband at the time, might be sticky about the custody issue. But he only cared about the money. I got total custody; he kept his money. We made a grand announcement of our divorce. That's how social we were, imagine. I went from James to Robert without a hitch."

Today, Nicole has been married to her lover for several years. Although her ex-husband is presently married also, Nicole says:

"My ex-husband and I are like best friends. Everyone said we'd get back together again. But James could never be a lover. He still represents what he did twenty years ago. He represents tradition. Shibboleths, which means he knows the right thing to do at the right time. He understands propriety, etiquette, old-world values. It still has an appeal for me. It will always appeal to me intellectually but I can't live with it—it doesn't hug or kiss or have passion. When I was looking to get married, I wanted to be written up in the New York Times. My announcement had to be written right, what they said about me. My lovers were not marriage material; their write-ups would not have been perfect. But they were passionate, wonderful men. But I didn't think that a person married a passionate, wonderful man. I thought that kind of man should only be the lover. Until I met Robert. Then I was able to make the transition with Robert. I was absolutely burning up with the fire when we were alone together, but he was appropriate in public too. His behavior was fine. So there I had lover and husband in one man. That was why I married him. I don't think I could have married an artist or starving musician. Those are the lovers only. I was lucky Robert proved to be both."

When asked what the biggest impact was, the real difference between Robert as the lover and James as the husband, Nicole immediately said it was the sex.

"Sex was phenomenally different. Different enough to make an impression. Let me put it this way. I have stick-straight hair and sex with Robert made my hair curl. Sex was the main reason for the relationship at first. I mean, it wasn't about having kids and it wasn't about marriage. It was about sex, pure and simple. Once we decided to be married, I made it clear that I did not want any more children. Children kill romance and I wanted to sustain that part of the affair with Robert. I wanted the sex to last."

During the period when Nicole spent time with Robert but remained married to James, she viewed her husband's behavior as "a very WASP approach" on most levels.

"If it was a Saturday night, it must be the night for sex. WASP men," Nicole sighs, "are not hot-blooded. I am multiorgasmic and if I can only have one, I won't be crabby, I'll be okay. But four or five are much better. By the fifth one I feel out of body. It's amazing. That's how it was from the beginning with Robert."

When Nicole did leave James for Robert, she describes Robert as "waiting in the wings."

"I probably would not have ever left James if not for Robert. But I can't say that he's the 'love of my life.' I don't know exactly what that means. If I see a handsome man, I still look. If someone winks across the room, I notice. The intrigue is fun, and *funny*. And love affairs are fun too. But a serious love affair is too much aggravation, too much remembering your lines. It's too complicated. To some women, if they aren't emotionally gratified in their marriage, maybe the intrigue of an affair is the part they get off on, but for me the intrigue made me nuts. I wanted to end it so I could move forward."

And that is why she married her other partner, Robert.

"I really believe that I could have married anyone, if I'd put my mind to it. I mean, what is in the marriage contract anyway? What's the deal? What do I do for you and what do you do for me? Women need to redefine marriage.

"After seven years [of being] married to Robert, who is so trustworthy, who hasn't stepped off the line once, I'd say he's a wonderful man. He promised me he'd never say no and he's kept his promise. He hasn't let me down. He's a wonderful, wonderful man. And he was from the start, when we were lovers."

When asked if she'd conduct an affair today, Nicole thinks not.

"Never in my life have I gone out looking for a man. I have a facility like a magnet, however, and there is some man who is always drawn to me. I throw off a vibe. But it doesn't mean I care. Usually I want to get away.

"Over the years my view of men has not changed, but I think my view of myself has changed. I'm less needy of their approval. In college I was needy of men. After all, we grew up in the fifties and sixties with *Pillow Talk*. It was such a colossal lie. I wanted to base my husband on a Rock Hudson. Imagine! I mean he was gay and it was all a lie. I never even heard the word orgasm until my mid-twenties, when I was already married. I was having them and I didn't know what to expect. People were virgins then, even if they were pregnant. People lived with lies like a veil. I was in search of the one woman who wasn't wearing the veil, who wasn't living the lie. Men wouldn't tell you the truth, or maybe they see it so differently, truth isn't the point. I wanted the superficial to disappear. Once the veil was parted for me, I knew I wasn't alone. Women friends are very important for women. Loving my women friends as I do, it helps. It helps because men are less important for the most part. That's the point. Put a bag on their heads and they're all about the same. That's how I feel now."

What is notable with Nicole is that she views sex as men often do; that is, when she dated in college, she would not have sex with an eligible man. Yet she was preoccupied with sex as reflected in the relationship with her lover; the sexual fluidity of the liaison was important.

In Nicole's case, the affair with its sexual aspect was most important; the relationship with her lover seems to be more about compelling sex than about the man. It was a big step for her. Despite her pull toward the traditional, she was able to follow her yearning to achieve something beyond the received female role.

In her case she was fortunate to find someone with whom she could blend her needs from both spheres. Her situation could even be described as wholesome; that is not always the case.

CR80

Kate

Kate, who is forty, grew up in a city in the Northeast and resides in another city in the Northeast. She was first married at the age of thirty and had known her spouse since she was twenty-two. They had an on-again, off-again relationship while attending college together.

The marriage was of short duration and it was then that she realized how attracted she was to other men. When asked why she married David, she told us she didn't know.

"From the night I got married, I knew it was wrong. I have no idea why I married David. Well, maybe because I never thought I'd meet anyone I'd really love. He was nice, and we were good friends. I stayed with him all the time because I never imagined I'd say good-bye to him."

She describes the marriage as more of a friendship than a love relationship. And throughout this period she was firmly entrenched in her career.

"I was an intern [medical student] when I got married and my career went full steam ahead no matter what. I was so intensely involved with my career that I'd not paid any attention to my personal life. There was no time. This took care of it neatly for me. He was a wonderfully nice guy, and I was undeveloped emotionally and socially. That's what happens to medical students, women medical students too. Anyway, David was never a person who wowed me. I think I married him partially to please my father. He wanted me to be married because he thought I was getting older and less desirable.

"My father had been a tremendous influence in my life. He was overbearing and sexist at the same time that he treated me as special. He was overly involved. I spoke with my father every day of my life until he died. And he influenced how I viewed women. I saw him put women down always; he viewed them as inferior. But because he was crazy about me I didn't feel like I was part of the female race he disparaged. I felt very special. I was always very smart and an achiever. But I was insecure with men always. It was once I had lovers, once I was married, that I began to feel desirable. I'd never felt so before."

When Kate was asked exactly what transpired after she and David were married, she told us that she "fell in love with a guy who was a resident at the same hospital."

"He was a year younger. I was madly in love with him and we had a wild affair with lots of sex and time spent together. It was terrific."

At that time she did not feel married to David, although she in fact was, and it was the very sensation that was her send-off for what followed.

"My first affair was incredible... I saw him every day. We went to breakfast together at the hospital and we had sex together in the hospital, often in the on-call rooms. We went to Vermont for a weekend, both of us lying to our partners to finesse it. I told David that I had to be on call and I never got caught. If this guy's apartment was empty during the week, we'd sometimes make love there as well. The sex was much better than with David and I began to not sleep with David after I began these affairs. My first lover wasn't married but he lived with someone. Although he was a shit, I would have left David in a minute for him. In fact one weekend my parents came up to visit and I had them take me to dinner and had this lover meet us there. There was such excitement in being with him. Yet the timing never worked. At first he was afraid to leave the woman he lived with. And then finally he did leave her. But by then it was too late, and I was onto Kyle, the lover who became my present husband. To this day the guy still calls me."

Kate describes the next lover, who preceded Kyle, as the one she thought she loved more than anyone else, someone she'd had a relationship with while she lived with David, before they were married. Kate tells us that had it worked out, life "would have been hellish."

"Yet he was the love of my life. Sex with him was the most wonderful experience. He was a thrilling man, in every way. The sex was unique, always different, always incredible. He hurt me, though, and I was bad. He was so handsome. The first one was less beautiful but this guy was unbelievable. The way men look, their physical appearance, is important to me. I've always been attracted to very handsome men."

It was then that Kate met the lover who became her present husband, Kyle. He was "wild, crazy, and full of energy" when they first met at the hospital where he was a lab technician and she was a resident. Initially she thought he was too young. Neither took the other seriously, but they began an affair anyway. Kate describes her first reaction to Kyle as one of suspicion.

"He was too handsome, even for me, too smooth. At this point I told David that I wanted a divorce. I was sleeping with Kyle all the time at his apartment. I began to feel sexual; I could demand good sex with my lover. I didn't sleep with David at all. I couldn't. We'd gotten counseling for a short period but I knew it was never going to work. I still remember the night we got married I wanted to wake up and discover it was all a dream. It was so awful because he was so nice, and he was devastated by me."

We asked Kate how Kyle as her lover reacted to everything going on.

"I think he trusted me right away. He understood that I just didn't love David. But I kept asking myself how he could trust me. I mean, if I did it to David, someone could do it to me. But I'd acted out of character, and I was so good at it. I lied and I conducted those affairs happily. And now here I am with Kyle, my last lover, who is seven years younger, and I ought to worry. I used to worry all the time. He's younger and he's so handsome. But I don't think of it anymore. I don't have time to worry now. I'm a terribly jealous person. When Kyle went away for a week to work and in his work he'd be with the most beautiful women in the world, I couldn't compete. I'm not one of those women. And so, I trust him. But it haunts me, that he knows what I did, so how could he trust me?"

Kate says she would not have an affair today because she is so madly in love with Kyle.

"But if I wasn't madly in love, it's an easy thing to do. Except if you have children. That's a big deal. I think that Kyle is the same as a husband as he was when we were lovers, except we don't get to see each other much with work and little kids. With Kyle everything is the greatest. And I know he's the right person because I used to watch every male who passed and I don't anymore. I mean, I take notice but I don't take action. Yet, I do remember my affair days as the most exciting time in my life. I only wish I hadn't hurt David. I thought it was a weakness on his part not to suspect me. I became too powerful and I didn't like that feeling."

Kate regards Kyle's role as her lover to have been the catalyst to set her free.

"I was a weak person. I had no social life as a resident, because no resident does, and I would have held on to David and what was easy. I might have had more lovers but I would have held on. I think I'm just lucky to have found Kyle."

Her career was always important to her. Only having children has made it less impacting.

"I never would have given up my career for a love affair but I would for my children. I haven't had to, though. I've made decisions but not sacrifices."

Her attitude toward men today has changed.

"It helped me understand men, having had love affairs. I never dated many people until I was married to David. It helped to see what is immoral. During that time I was immoral, or should I say amoral. But I had to do it for me. My life is very solid right now. Kyle and the children are the most important part of my life. It is my passion to instill right and wrong into my children. I think it is because as an adult I did something immoral in having lovers while married. Yet I'd be forever curious if I hadn't tried things. It didn't even feel like me when it happened, like it wasn't my personality. Now I've come full cycle. I have this naive conception that I never ever want to be with anyone else besides Kyle. With my lovers, sex was so important–the proof of it really counted. I felt very sexual at the time. And then I met Kyle, and he was my lover. It was Kyle, not marriage, that settled me down."

For Kate, the interaction with her lovers was a reaction to feeling trapped both in her marriage and within her own life. Because she found someone who returned her love, after suffering disappointments with various men, she was able to leave her husband and to break her pattern. Kate felt deprived, almost as if she were a teenager, and once married, she seemed to revert to adolescence. Kate "dated" while being married almost as a teenager plays the field. This phase was a revival of adolescence.

ⱌⱄ

Edwina

Edwina comes from a large family and is forty years old. She grew up in a suburb of a midwestern city, where she now lives. Her parents divorced during her childhood and her first comments related to the known fact that children of divorce and affairs tend to repeat their parents' patterns. She sees herself as no exception and believes that her parents clearly functioned as her role models. Edwina, presently divorced, is the mother of two children and engaged to be married a second time.

"I was first married at nineteen to a man I'd known since I was fifteen, someone I met at a pre-deb party in the city. We were set up and married soon after. I felt railroaded from the beginning. I also felt very secure; our families were friends and we led a nice life. But I realized very early on that I'd made a huge mistake. I cared for him a great deal, sort of like an errant sibling. We were never really in love, but I'm still protective of him today, even when he continues to behave badly." Behaving "badly" refers to a problem with alcohol, which Edwina says is what finally drove her away. At that time she was not interested in other men but preoccupied with the failing marriage and her second pregnancy.

"I had a business and we had our families, which were connected. I decided to stay with him because I had a busy life. If I stayed with him for a few more years, it might be better for the children. We were on a fast track socially, lots of parties, you know. And then I met this man. I met him with his wife at a party and I was drawn to him. We lived in the same town; we knew a lot of the same people. He was unhappily married also, although I didn't know it at the time. I only knew that I was drawn to him. We were intellectually compatible and physically compatible. We began talking on the phone, being a support system for each other. It came as a surprise to me when we had a sexual relationship. I'd decided long ago that I wasn't going to have an affair with anyone. Then it happened. It was an amazing part of the relationship. The sex really counted and was nothing like my experience in my marriage. I tried to resist; I couldn't. It was off again, on again for years. We saw each other almost daily, even if just for a walk or a kiss good-night. For nine years we spoke on the phone a few times a day."

When asked where she and her lover would meet, Edwina explained how careful they were, how afraid of causing a scandal.

"We'd meet downtown. We had special places, but were extremely cautious because both of us were still married and we actually disapproved of what we were doing but it was out of our control. We were very much a product of our social upbringing. We were worried about hurting our mates but compelled to be together. When I was with him I was elevated to another level."

Finally Edwina decided she couldn't remain in her marriage any longer. Facing a failed marriage was not easy for her.

"I got my husband to move out. We'd been in and out of therapy at this point but it was obvious that there was no way. He really was an alcoholic. We were beyond help. My husband gave me sole custody. I traded on his wealth. He was very wealthy. I wanted the children and he kept his money. I had no skills. I was raised to have breakfast in bed, you know? So I moved the kids to the wrong side of town and I began a new life."

Edwina was with her lover throughout her divorce but once she was divorced, her expectations changed.

"I didn't want to be the mistress of a married man. He couldn't leave his children—he had two children the same age as mine. It was horrible. We loved each other and I waited. He always said he'd leave when his children were a certain age. I always believed him."

Yet she was not unhappy being divorced, despite the unresolved nature of her lover's situation. She describes this time period as "lots of fun." Although she didn't date anyone else, she watched her divorced friends date only younger men, and she waited, waited for her lover to be free.

When asked about the sexual aspect of their relationship at this juncture, Edwina admits they were still engaged in "off-again, on-again" sex.

"I always wanted to have sex with him. The physical attraction was so strong it frightened me. But I wanted to be sure nothing was jeopardized now that I was free. While we were both married, I was preoccupied with the affair in a different way. An affair is like having an occupation. You spend your time getting ready, covering for where you're going, making excuses for what you're doing. Then getting back to your real life and winding down at the end of the time together. And it was worth it for me. Although all your life is duplicitous. I cut out friends because I couldn't make the time and because I couldn't share it with them, this major part of my life that was such a secret. It's amazing, though, how women who have affairs recognize one another immediately, like a secret pact. If my lover and I were together at a party, women who had affairs would come over to me later and say, 'I know what you're going through.' They understood. I think it's how some women survive, by understanding each other. Even if women have husbands and/or lovers, it's not enough. If a man is powerful, most of his life is wrapped up in his work. They aren't available, be it as a lover or as a husband. They aren't there for you. Women are."

Edwina's lover decided to get divorced ahead of schedule after a particular incident.

"Several years ago, I went to a sports event with a younger fellow and a bunch of guys. My lover called three or four times a day, at a minimum. Anyway, I didn't reach him to tell him I'd be out and he went nuts. He called my house every five minutes for two hours straight. The next morning at dawn he appeared to check the house, to make sure I hadn't slept with anyone the night before. Soon after, he left his wife. I felt terrible for him because I knew our lives wouldn't change immediately, that it wouldn't be easy. There was a struggle ahead but he was happy he'd decided to leave. I waited while he established himself. It was still a sticky situation with his children and wife. And then I became very ill, seriously ill. He stuck by me while I was sick."

Today, Edwina and her lover are living together as they wait for his divorce to come through. They've purchased a large house and while Edwina says she is "still madly in love with him," she also admits, "He's a pain in the ass, like most men. High-powered, egotistical, in the money world."

"There's no question that it's still the same mad passion, ten years later. He's the love of my life. Yet he's no less difficult than any man. That's what I know today in my limited experience but with a new vision. In the previous marriages he and I were the capable ones, so now it's very competitive between us. We both like to take charge."

Edwina describes her "bliss" as circumscribed.

"As my lover, in the beginning, I recognized we shared the same goals, values and standards. That was enormously important. Yet, there are certain things I can never have because of him. We like different sports, have different ways of living our lives. It doesn't really hit you as lovers but as potential spouses, it is definitely there, the compromising."

When asked if she felt that perhaps she'd closed out other chances, with other men, she admitted she did.

"Men are never a problem. There are always available men. I

believe any woman can walk out the door and have a flirtation, or an affair. My idea is that the game is to really have someone wonderful and to keep him. There are incredible twenty-four-year-old women after him and it drives me nuts. Here I am forty, getting over an illness. And that's when I remember I was naive. I had other opportunities I didn't recognize at the time. So I know any woman can have affairs along the way."

Edwina used her connection with her lover to get out of her marriage. Even though the affair provided this escape, it came with its own set of problems. The problems were substantial, and her fantasy of being rescued by a sexual/spiritual man has only been partly satisfied. Her lover will become her husband and she will face the serious and mundane aspects of life with him. She seems to understand full well that she has shifted out of the honeymoon phase of their intimacy.

We see Edwina as convention-bound with a twist, the twist being her early exposure to her parents' divorce and her feeling that she was unable to escape a similar fate. In repeating the pattern, she is familiar with the pitfalls yet she chooses to go forward, entering a second marriage. Her point of view is that marriage is what is acceptable by society's standards and therefore the only choice.

CRED

Laura

Laura, thirty-eight, describes her childhood in Australia as quite ordinary. As was expected, she was educated in England and lived there the early years of her marriage. She was married at twenty for the first time, and the marriage lasted sixteen years and produced a child. For eleven years of her marriage, Laura lived a "respectable" life in Boston. Meeting her lover, who became her present husband, was the first break from tradition that she ever experienced.

Although she describes she and her ex-husband as "best friends today," Laura admits that she and Andrew do not discuss her current relationship on any level. Mostly their conversations revolve around their twelve-year-old daughter and their joint custody. When asked about her lover, Laura chose to begin with the topic of her previous marriage.

"First let me say how I saw my marriage. We came from identical backgrounds, the same religion. Our families knew each other for centuries. While I won't say it was an arranged marriage, I would say that we were encouraged to marry each other. Andrew is eight years older than I, and I was very young when we married. I think of that marriage as a pair of beautiful shoes. While they were never comfortable, I would do everything in my power to make them so. It was as if I tried Band-Aids, suffered through the blisters, had them stretched to fit until finally I said, forget it, enough.

"And yet I believe my marriage was better than ninety percent of all marriages. What we had was parallel play, like children. We lived together and did our own thing, side by side, not together. I certainly didn't want to reach sixty that way. It was definitely a reflection of the marriage that we did not have any more children together and I spent a great deal of my time at work. I had a high-powered job, especially in the eighties. At various times during the marriage we talked about separating, so when I did tell Andrew that I actually wanted to split up, the shock was not about a separation but that there was another man. His initial reaction was that because I'd been married so young, it was all right if I sowed my wild oats and then returned to him. In other words, have an affair if I had to, but don't leave the marriage. It seemed very noble at the time, but it wasn't what I wanted to do. I had found someone and I was ready to make my move."

Laura and her lover, Kenneth, met during a business transaction.

He was married at the time as well and lived in the countryside, an hour outside of the city.

"He was also European but came from a completely different background, and is such a completely different man than Andrew. Maybe that's the draw. I never looked at Kenneth as an alternative, though–never. He was the man I chose as my lover. That was how it began.

"What happened was that six months after our first meeting, Kenneth asked me to have dinner to discuss the project. I told him I was married and had a child and that I didn't do dinner, but I'd do a lunch. I even ran it by Andrew. I said to him I'd met this success-ful money manager and he'd asked me to dinner. Andrew said why not go, because he knew that there were contacts, people this man knew who would help my business. He knew how important my work was to me. So Kenneth and I went to one of the most elegant restaurants and had a super dinner together. I kept thinking through-out the evening, if ever I wanted an affair, Kenneth was the man. After all, he was from an opposite world from my Upper East Side existence; we knew no one in common. I figured that our lives would never cross; no one in my circle would know him. And he seemed so worldly and smooth, although I know now it's not the case at all.

"I realized I wanted the affair. It began immediately. There was sex, elegant dates, restaurants, hotels. He courted me and I adored it. I remember it was the beginning of Desert Storm when we started. In the midst of everything turning upside down, it was a perfect affair. I could think of little else. It was all that I ever expected it to be. We met during the day for romantic interludes. The sex was fabulous."

Describing how she felt about her husband and child during this interval, Laura says, "One does feel schizophrenic while it's going on. And I felt very guilty looking at Andrew and at my daughter those nights. All I could think of was Kenneth. There was a high degree of integrity in my marriage and we were decent to one another; there was no shouting or abuse. So I felt guilty. I wondered how to untangle my life, our lives. We had our friends and family, who we loved. There was a lot at stake."

However, Laura pursued the relationship with Kenneth and was "immersed."

"Soon the affair was in full swing. I'd gone to Europe to a spa with two friends and I'd agreed to meet Kenneth for the last three days while my friends went on. When I saw him I said that I couldn't lie like this, that I'm a nice Jewish girl and it had gone too far. In the meantime, he'd gotten separated. I found it easier when we were both married, so he threw me a curve ball by getting separated. The context of the relationship was different once he was 'single' and I wasn't. And then he was divorced in two months' time. It all happened so quickly. His ex-wife and children moved abroad. Then I realized I'd begun to fall in love. Kenneth was so supportive and kind, so generous. It was that kind of courtship—romance, sex, passion. Everything. It was almost frighteningly good in every way."

Laura admits that part of the attraction was how opposite Kenneth was to Andrew.

"For instance, Andrew was always calling me a spendthrift and worried I'd spend all the money, that there'd be none left. This relationship with Kenneth is the opposite. He sees my mode as conservative. I don't know if it's the buttons one presses or that each person is so different. I felt appreciated and very special with Kenneth from the start."

Today Laura and her lover are married and she is expecting a child in several weeks. She is presently living in the town where Kenneth had lived before they met. Together they are building a home and she is "extremely happy" with her new life.

Laura feels she was fortunate to have embarked upon a "true love affair" even if she and Kenneth had not married.

"It was worth the risk, worth the guilt and worth the scandal. The way I see it, some affairs break up marriages; some women return to their spouse in a better frame of mind. Half of the people in my business are having affairs. It isn't only men who have affairs but women too. After all, who are these men having affairs with, only their single secretaries? Not at all. I know that for a fact. There are so many people out there having them. I understand that although it was awful to lead a secret life, it was wonderful to have an affair with Kenneth. I was happy to be with him. And ultimately he changed everything, my entire existence.

"I believe that women have affairs because there is something in their marriage which is lacking–boredom sets in or they are no longer in love with their husbands. It gave me a whole new life. I regrouped and emerged richer. I'm very lucky that the magic continues."

It seems that Laura was able to use the relationship as a way to leave her marriage. While she did not initially plan it that way, the tryst with her lover became an all-encompassing affair. Physically and emotionally connected to this man, she was uncomfortable with their secret meetings.

Once she knew she was in love, she was better able to accept her actions. For her, the idea of a lover was not appealing or exciting, but part of the realization that she no longer wished to be married to Andrew. Traditional in her upbringing, Laura struggled with her divorce and the concepts of a new marriage and the move to a new town. However, once the break was made and she began anew, she was happy. Her relationship with her lover/ new spouse represents another chance, without compromises.

∞

Lucia

Lucia is thirty-eight years old and lives in Arizona, having grown up in Colorado. Her childhood was "very normal and suburban."

She was married for the first time at the age of twenty-two, a marriage which lasted for nine years. She describes the marriage as having had "incredible extremes."

"My first husband was a substance abuser, which I think is the earmark of a failed first marriage. I simply did not understand that it was a chronic problem, and I lived an insane up-and-down existence. The real-life stuff got in the way of our passions. Things like having a child to consider–this proved an interference for a marriage like ours.

"But once we did have a child, my level of tolerance changed and I was no longer willing to put up with my husband's pattern. We separated several times, but actually stayed together for ages."

During the marriage, when her child was quite young, Lucia met a man who became her lover. The relationship lasted for five years.

"We met on a job location. We were in the same business. He was very different than my husband and several years older. He had a few kids and we began to talk to each other by talking about our children–that was the common bond. There weren't many married people on the job and we were both away from home. It was a long-distance affair. He was living at a hotel and away from his family when it began. I think I was drawn to him because he picked up on my neediness, my need to be comforted."

The attraction for Lucia was not physical but intensely emotional.

"He was persistent and comforting, a solid person, dependable, reassuring, responsible. He was all that you can't get from an alcoholic husband. That was the thing for me.

"We arranged to see each other as often as possible. If we were on a job together, it was great. Depending on my work schedule I would see him fourteen hours a day, other times not for a month at a time. But we always were trying to see each other. We agreed from the start that neither of us would ever get divorced. We felt committed to our marriages. Then I fell in love with him. I began to compare what I had with what I could have. My marriage appeared unhealthy, although having an affair with a married man wasn't wholesome either. But he was, my lover was, wholesome and good.

"We really loved each other. After one week we knew it would continue. He was serious about the fact that he would never be divorced. Yet we were out of control and schemed to be together constantly. He wanted to protect his family. My husband and I were deteriorating by then. I always knew enough, though, to avoid making demands upon my lover. It would never have achieved the result I wanted.

"I felt like there were times when I was so desperate to be with him that I'd go nuts. I think that having an affair is a prescription to go nuts. Instead I got an ulcer. I was involved with two men at once but I only wanted the lover."

Lucia decided to get divorced after a particular incident.

"When my husband returned from a business trip he had an accident. This changed my plans. I was with my lover when I learned about it and I knew I couldn't leave my husband, that I had to take care of him, despite the state of the marriage. And I did. I suppose I was still trying to work it out on some level with my husband. I reentered the typical chaos of his life. Then I realized that I had to be divorced."

For Lucia, the affair offered her a "perspective on what life would be like" with a man who would make her happy. Yet she made several attempts to keep her marriage together before finally leaving

"I found it ironic that I was with someone who cheated and still cared about not hurting his wife and family. That was what I wanted, without the cheating.

"I wanted the love I had in the affair in a marriage. In retrospect, my husband was a liar and most likely a cheat. I felt I had to confront my husband and explain that I didn't respect or love him. I eased him into the divorce. My lover was so supportive and listened to me, all day long at work. I was in that period when I was able to see him for twelve or fourteen hours a day. I had a full-time babysitter and rarely saw my child. It was a crazy time for me, not something I'm proud of.

"Then I met someone else and I began to see both men, my lover and this new man, and I was separating from my husband. The marriage was an intense, on-again, off-again marriage until it truly ended. Eventually I married the new man, and he is my present husband."

In looking back at her relationship with her married lover, Lucia has no regrets.

"It was complicated but it helped me. The sex with the lover was never as good as in my first marriage, nor as good as in my second marriage. But if the sex was mediocre, the love part was so important and so immediate, that it worked. Both husbands have been better sexually, though. Whatever made this lover happy made me happy, that was how it was. Usually sex is a big issue and here the needs were different. We had another kind of hold on each other. I'd never met a person of that ilk. The attraction was of another order.

"Once I told him I was seeing someone else (the man who became my second husband), he carried on. I never said, 'But you're with someone, you're with your wife, so why can't I be with someone, now that I'm separated?' He went so far as to say he didn't want to sleep with me at that point, but it didn't last."

What finally ended Lucia's attachment to her other partner was her engagement to her second husband.

"I broke it off but I wanted to remain friends. I had depended on his calling me and he stopped completely. I missed hearing from him. I now get word through friends but I didn't think he'd stop being in touch altogether."

Today Lucia feels that her life is "in order" and that she is "an adult again." She would not pursue a relationship outside the marriage or jeopardize what she has at this stage.

Lucia's interaction with her lover was a direct reaction to serious marital problems. Her lover provided a refuge, an escape from a poor marriage. The romance seems to have been very security-oriented without much passion.

The relationship with the lover also offered an escape from the demands and drains of mothering. Lucia, in fact, used the lover to create another life because her own became intolerable. With time she was able to use it as a means of transition to a new marital relationship.

Despite the severity of Lucia's problems within her marriage, she hung on to it and remained with the lover. Her dependency needs were very strong, as if she had not learned to be on her own. Finally, she broke free and began anew.

ॐ

Bridget

Bridget grew up in Orange County, California. From a "blue-collar" family, she married by the time she was twenty and had children immediately. Her mother had also married young and had children quickly. Bridget believed she was "doing the right thing." However, her training was in nursing and when her children were school-age, she secured a job near her home.

"I would describe my marriage as decent. My husband is very much like my family. He is a blue-collar worker who takes his job seriously and is a good family man. I stopped thinking about why I'd first been with him, after a while. The kids kept me busy and I was waiting for the day when I could return to work and have a life of my own.

"I began to work for a pediatrics practice. It was a very busy office and I liked that. I really welcomed the change. One of the doctors on the staff went out of his way to be nice to me from the very first day. We began to have lunch together and he started to show an interest in me.

"One day he told me that I should dress better and color my hair. He wanted me to wear finer clothes and on a Saturday he actually showed me some stores that sold the 'right' clothes. He bought books for me and wanted me to read them so that we could discuss them. He would recommend films for me to see. None of these things pleased my husband, of course. Not the books or movies or even the clothes."

What got Bridget's husband's attention was when she began to dress differently and to attend plays and museums in Los Angeles.

"He was absolutely furious. He really resented the changes in me, and my independence. I think he mostly disliked that I could have other interests in life.

"At about the same time, this doctor and I were riding together in his car from one office to the other when he propositioned me. I said no, that I couldn't possibly get involved. I felt very confused and I knew that I wanted to. I was worried about breaking the rules and about my marriage. I didn't want to cause any trouble but I was really attracted to this man. After work that day we made love on one of the examining tables. It was very satisfying. We began a routine of having sex at the end of the workday and we would order Chinese food afterward."

Bridget fell madly in love with her lover.

"I was crazy about him. I thought about him constantly and I wanted to be more attached. At first I didn't mention my feelings to him but after a while I felt I had to. After a year and a half, I told him I thought he ought to leave his wife and I would leave my husband. This doctor did not want any part of it. We continued to make love but I had a specific night and we did not do it on the other nights, only on schedule. I didn't question that. I knew the sex was wonderful and I was in love. What more was there to do if he wasn't going to leave his wife?

"The more strident I became about our leaving our marriages, the more this doctor wanted to extricate himself from our affair. He became very uninterested in our relationship, which was devastating to me. I wanted more from it. I thought I was going to spend the rest of my life with this man."

The affair ended when Bridget discovered her lover with someone else.

"I was scheduled to work in the evening at one of the branch offices. When I arrived, there were no patients in the office. There was my lover with a nurse from the practice. They were on one of the examining tables exactly as we did it. I couldn't believe it. I was devastated. I was absolutely heartbroken.

"The next day I quit my job and found another one quite fast. It is in another medical office, but I will never turn my head to look at one of the doctors. As far as this relationship goes, I learned about the arts and, I admit, I did learn how to dress and to improve my appearance. I also learned that he never loved me and that this was his way of doing things. I was one of many, which sickens me. I still keep up with theater, art and music. That was the gift that lasts. And my husband is interested in culture because I am. He's sort of joined me in my new venture, and that helps the marriage. I'm relieved I didn't jump the gun and leave my husband. I compare him to my lover and he appears to be a nicer man. Now I am pleased to be with him. I think he's a good husband and he stands by me. The affair taught me that what I have is worth having. I'm not sorry about the affair and I'm fortunate it didn't become a complete disaster."

Bridget was dissatisfied with her life and her marriage when she resisted, then welcomed the love affair with the doctor. She was naive about the kind of situation it was and the kind of man the doctor might have been.

Perhaps she thought herself "in love" with her lover in order to justify the relationship. In a sense, she was saved from a calamity by her lover's rejection of her. Because she did not move out of her marriage, it was still there for her. She was able to take what she learned about culture and sophistication with her. Her husband has met her at some juncture and together they enjoy the experience that Bridget's lover brought to her life. She seems grateful and ready to be with her husband and family completely.

CঙৎꝚ

Jessica

Jessica, a thirty-three-year-old attorney, lives in the Baltimore suburb where she grew up. Her childhood was "quite normal" and she was always self-motivated and extroverted. Although promiscuous in high school, she married at twenty-two and did not have much contact with other men as an adult. Her marriage lasted nine years.

"My husband James was handsome and easygoing, but a cold fish. I married him when I was too young and we stayed together until I was thirty-one. He came from a completely different background than mine. It was not until the end of the marriage that I realized we'd grown apart. But I was not prepared to break off the relationship. He was a computer scientist and I was a law student. We were not the least bit interested or involved in each other's careers.

"When I landed my first job after law school, I met my lover. He was separated at the time and neither of us had children. We were only encumbered by our marital situations and he was on his way out of his. He was ten years older and a senior partner, a very important guy at the firm.

"The first attraction was our mutual profession. I was very en-thusiastic about the work and my lover was very experienced in what I was interested in. He had a position of power and I liked that. He was very cerebral and animated, while my husband was not. My husband was cold and remote, not unfriendly, but very detached. I loved the power and knowledge my lover had; I was seduced by it."

The actual affair began when Jessica and her lover were working on a case together.

"We were staying out late and were working constantly. Then we'd have a late dinner. After two or three glasses of wine we were no longer talking about the case but openly flirting. He invited me back to his place. I was very attracted to him. We began a private and secretive affair in the office. I felt guilty about James, and at the same time there was a lot of going back and forth in my mind. I realized after three months with my lover that I didn't love James and that I loved the lover. I was ready to jump from one marriage to the next but there was no affirmation from my lover. He gave me no hint that he wanted me to divorce James for him. I was too afraid to sacrifice the security of the marriage, and ten years of my life."

The time that Jessica shared with her lover was spent at his place to have sex.

"We had no social life and we saw nobody because it was a big secret. We cooked in his apartment but he didn't even have a VCR so we weren't able to watch movies. When I returned to my place, I was still sleeping with James but it was so different from the sex with my lover.

"Sex with James was basically screwing, something we did be-fore we went to bed, after David Letterman. It was a routine like doing the dishes. It was Letterman, brush your teeth, sex. James did not like oral sex and didn't want to do it. He wanted me to do it to him, though. I didn't know this bothered me until after I had the affair. Then I realized how I felt about it. Once I had my lover I questioned how happy I was and what it was I was in search of.

"With my lover, the sex was much more original. There was a chemical attraction and the actual sex lasted longer. But I continued to sleep with my husband because I was only able to see my lover two times a week and because I hadn't made the break."

Jessica's lover bought her gifts and "seemed serious."

"The affair lasted for three months before I began to campaign for more of a commitment. During that time, my lover bought me negligees and bustiers, which made the sex exciting. We took showers together; he'd shave my pubic hair. The relationship became serious sexwise and emotionally. That was why I wanted the commitment in hand. Once I had it, I waited several months more and then I left my husband. He was so undemonstrative a person that when I said I don't want to be married and I'm moving out, he didn't even ask where I was going or with whom."

At this point, Jessica was "confused" about her attachments, and when her husband's father died, she traveled with him to attend the funeral.

"I tried to be his friend but he didn't need it. And by then I was living with my lover. We had no kids together, James and I, so it should have been a clean break. After that, with some legal arrangements to discuss, we rarely spoke. That made it easier to move forward with my lover. My husband always expected me to return to him, no matter how the divorce proceeded, but I didn't. By the time I moved in with my lover, his divorce had come through. I was officially divorced soon after and within days of that, I married my lover.

"I realize now that I never really had any time by myself as an adult. I went from a college dorm roommate to my first husband to my second husband. I never had but a day or two when I was unmarried."

Presently, Jessica feels very pleased with the decision she made.

"I'm pregnant with our baby and I've really settled down. But always there is a question of trust about my lover who became my husband. I guess when one begins a clandestine relationship, the trust is precarious. Maybe I'm feeling vulnerable as my belly grows because I know he's wandered before."

Jessica is fortunate in that she was able to move from one relationship to the next so easily. She wanted another kind of man in her life and her lover fit the bill. The fact that it worked out so smoothly is somewhat unusual. It seems that her love affair was a relationship that now sustains the day-to-day demands of married life. While Jessica is conventional in her approach to men, she was courageous enough to conduct the relationship with her lover and to leave the security for a man she loved. But Jessica has nagging doubts about a husband who was formerly a lover. For her, as for others, this is a compelling issue.

self-esteem

affairs

4

Self-Esteem Affairs

INTRODUCTION BY DR. JANE BLOOMGARDEN

Dr. Jane Bloomgarden received her Ph.D. at New York University Graduate School of Arts and Sciences. She has a postdoctoral degree in psychoanalysis and psychotherapy from NYU. Presently she is a supervisor at Yeshiva University's graduate program and on staff at White Plains Hospital, Children's Division. She has a private practice in the New York area.

Like other experts I've interviewed, Dr. Bloomgarden believes that each woman who embarks on an extramarital affair has her own particular set of reasons for doing so. However, she also recognizes a growing cultural trend away from marriage as a sacrosanct institution.

"There are specific circumstances which can trigger a woman's decision to engage in a sexual relationship outside the marriage. One is when the marriage embodies the past she may be trying to reject, even while feeling bound to it. Difficult or unhappy relationships with significant people in her past may have either conditioned her choice of a husband or may allow her to experience that husband, without very much basis, as being just like the people she sought to escape from when she married. By remaining in their marriages and seeking a lover outside the marriage, these women make their outer lives the representation of their inner conflict: they do not forsake their original families for the company of their lovers. Their ambivalence about leaving their marriages is schematized by their double life.

"A second situation I have noted is when a woman genuinely experiences a changing definition of self. Her marriage may then be experienced as restrictive and demeaning. The view of her husband as someone who is at odds with her growth causes her to seek other people who may endorse her development. Seeking a lover may answer her need for endorsement from another, when endorsement is denied her in her own home. Ibsen's *A Doll's House* is one stunning account of a marriage that has failed to grow, with a woman striving for personal development.

"The third syndrome is that which *Madame Bovary* immortalizes. Like Emma Bovary, a woman may be personally and profoundly dissatisfied. She looks to a man for what she lacks in herself, engaging in an affair for the sake of putting an end to her experience of inner poverty. She acts upon affairs as a means of finding inner satisfaction, hoping they can resolve her sense of emptiness and misery. But such solutions are never more than transiently successful. With so profound a need, it would be impossible for any one person to fill her sense of inner desolation. Her husband's tragedy was in loving her when she herself had no experience of being able to love or be loved. She could only love men from a distance, men who were idealized and narcissistically disposed. Unable to love a man who loved her, she rejected her husband and treated him as an unnecessary nuisance.

"A fourth common theme in the psychodynamics of extramarital affairs would seem to be the desire to score a victory in what is traditionally called 'the Oedipal situation.' Some women may venture outside their own marriages to triumphantly engage another woman's husband. A history of competition between mother and daughter and an overvaluation of the man as trophy in their strivings for personal recognition and value often underlie such pursuits. Sometimes women who pursue such affairs are interested in forging new relationships gained from such a victory, but not always. Sometimes they prefer to sustain a triangle, other wives or lovers included, in the interests of replicating those interpersonal rivalries which occupied them as children. Then, living with a mother and a father who engaged in highly charged and competitive relationships, they were one point in a triangle founded on the concepts of winning and losing, wanting their fathers and wanting to be wanted by them, even in the presence of mothers who would compete with them and resent them for their participation."

Dr. Bloomgarden recognizes a genuine desire to end a marriage as another reason that some women engage in affairs.

"Afraid to be alone, some women attach themselves to new men in the interest of leaving an unsatisfactory marriage. But some women are reluctant to leave a poor marriage even with the help of a lover. Sometimes women are afraid to hurt their marriage partner, and sometimes they are afraid of being hurt by them should they act on their desire to leave.

"Other reasons also may operate when a woman chooses to sustain her marriage and involves herself with a lover at the same time. Some women are fearful of intimacy, and manage to titrate their experience of closeness by never relying on just one man. Sustaining both involvements can also defend against fears of closeness based on injurious or threatening experiences in the past. Some women avoid the fear of possible rejection by any one man by sustaining relationships with more than one at a time.

"Having an affair can also be a way of expressing hostility and seeking to assert power in the marriage. Instead of directly dealing with her resentment of her husband's actions or attitudes, a woman may seek to attack her husband through an affair."

What Dr. Bloomgarden reminds us is how specific each situation is.

"We need to remember that each woman has her own life story. Motivations and reasons are individual and subjective. Sometimes affairs can be useful in the development of an individual. Sometimes they are symptoms of deeper problems that need to be better understood in order to make a real contribution to a woman's development."

CR80

Allegra

Allegra, who is forty and divorced, had an affair five years ago with her college boyfriend. While he was the incentive to leave her marriage, she is not with him today. Recently she became engaged to a man she met through the workplace.

"I had an affair with my college boyfriend ten years into my marriage," says Allegra. "I never expected this to happen, but he and I met unexpectedly at a party. He called me a few months later and asked me to lunch. Both of us were married and we each had two kids—I had just had a baby. We began to meet every few weeks and I knew that I still loved him. When we were together, it was safe and comfortable and I was happy. This made me see how unhappy I'd been in my marriage, and for so many years. The truth is, we had lost touch and I had married on the rebound. So after two children and a house in the suburbs, I found myself sneaking off to the city to meet my boyfriend.

"For a while it was perfect, and I lived for those days when I could see him. We were on the phone constantly and we had phone dates. I would usually call his cell while I was waiting for my son at a sports event. We saw each other as often as we could. I was really bending in half to be with him. We met at hotels and at empty apartments, wherever it was possible.

"After almost two years, I decided to get a divorce and my lover understood. He knew that my marriage was no good and he was my support system during the entire ordeal. I leaned on him and he was there, but he never spoke of the future. I began to see that I was getting divorced for myself and not for him. But he had given me the strength to do it, and the confidence that I could go out in the world again. I was so beaten down by my marriage, which was such a sham. I remember that I would go to parties with my husband and I would be missing my lover. I would call him. Sometimes he'd answer his cell and he'd be with his wife and kids at a restaurant. It began to upset me, and I felt tainted. Why were we doing something so fundamentally dishonest and ugly? Whether he wanted a divorce from his wife or not, I wanted to be free.

"After my divorce I saw how much I needed to be with my lover and how I had to face that he was not going to be there, except to meet on occasion. He wasn't going to leave his wife for me, and as much as I wanted him to leave, I also wanted it to be for himself, not for me. Finally, after six months, he told me he was almost certain that he wanted to leave the marriage. By then I was really nuts, a single mother trying to hold it together. I was bewildered and uncertain of the world, and while I was relieved to be divorced, I knew I wanted a full life, not an affair. My lover's wife became pregnant and that was when I told him I couldn't do anything else. I told him it wasn't going to work. He said he would still leave, but I couldn't face any more of it. It was too complicated and I'd already broken up one family. I saw what affairs and divorce can do to people and I didn't want him to go through with it. I never saw him as strong enough anyway. That was the irony—he gave me strength, but he wasn't really very strong.

"Today I am about to marry a man who I really love. He does not have a wife, just an ex-wife. He does not have a story, he's just a regular person. It is so much cleaner and healthier for me. But I can't honestly say that I don't think of my lover who I loved so much. There are days when he comes to mind and I tell myself that the timing was never right. I am thrilled to be with my future husband, who is kind and understanding. What I love most about him, after a bad marriage and an affair, is the fact that his story is so uncomplicated. He's simply there for me, without needing a reservation in an hotel to make it happen."

It seems that Allegra's lover provided a way to admit how unhappy her marriage was. While she regained her self-esteem through the affair and recovered from a bad situation, she chose not to continue the affair without any promise of a future. Had her lover been able to extricate himself, it is likely that they would have ended up together. Since this was not possible, and the facts were complicated by children, Allegra made the decision to do what was best for her. In a sense, the affair was a stepping stone to her present and future. And while it seems she loved this man, she was true to herself in not insisting he divorce and marry her. In the end, she was able to find happiness elsewhere.

CRUD

Amanda

Amanda is a physician. She practices full-time. She grew up in St. Louis and spent most of her married life in Texas. She has been married for thirteen years and has no children. She is close to forty and her husband is approaching fifty.

Although Amanda feels her marriage has "improved" in the past year and a half, since she and her husband have been seeing a therapist, she assures me it "has not been restored to wonderful."

"The therapy has definitely helped and we've resolved certain problems, but both my husband and I have sustained relationships outside the marriage. I attribute these to a breakdown in our relationship. On the other hand, we belong to the same church, where we both serve as deacons, which is a big part of our life and a common bond."

Amanda's experience with her lover was a result of her husband's infidelities.

"My husband has had several flings and finally I decided that if he is so afraid to completely commit himself, then it was acceptable for me to do the same. I'd have to say that my affair was a reaction to my husband's behavior.

"This man was a doctor at the same hospital where I worked and we saw each other constantly. Maybe nine hours a day. I remember that when I first met him, I found him very attractive but he was married. I was single at the time, and I assumed he was unavailable. We became very friendly and the friendship was solid, an enjoyable one. Once I was open to the concept of having an affair, I realized that he was indeed available, marriage or no marriage. By then he had children as well, but none of this seemed to matter to him.

"It didn't go well from the start. It was the physical aspect of the relationship that I found to be difficult. As soon as this man became more than a friend, it was a conflict. I was continually aware of my status and my involvement with my husband. I suppose I had difficulty with the concept of sustaining two physical relationships at the same time."

When asked about the sex, Amanda tells us that it was "not great."

"The sex was not as good as with my husband. Perhaps I wasn't comfortable with this man, but I was very attracted to him. As a lover he was not as interested in taking care of me as my husband was. That was what I was accustomed to and I preferred it that way.

However, I continually expected the sex with my lover to improve and so I pursued it.

"I was emotionally involved with my lover. That was where the disappointment occurred. He made a big deal of telling me that I was his first infidelity and later on I learned that he had lied about that. He told me I was special and a departure but he had in fact conducted other affairs. I resented being relegated to the same category as these other affairs because we'd been friends first. And because he attempted to fool me.

"Mostly we had sex at the hospital. We sneaked around to empty rooms and went to a motel once. That was pretty tacky. We spent so much time together in the hospital, it was quite easy to pull off. There are many affairs that transpire in medical centers and in hospitals. It's such a pressured environment, sex is a relief and a release. I see it all the time with nurses and doctors and secretaries. Doctors married to nonmedical people, as I am, especially fall into this category. I suppose the common bond of the medical world provides the basis for the other relationship to foster.

"While the affair was going on I did not feel that my marriage was in jeopardy. My approach was quite different. I made it clear to my husband that the affair was in full swing to drive home my point that what was acceptable for him was acceptable for me as well. I also think it was partly the 'honesty in marriage' theory that provoked my confession. It bothered my husband more than he let on. He was also a proponent of the double standard. Deep down it bothered him, I'm sure of it."

After several months, Amanda's affair with the doctor ended and she "regrouped in terms of the marriage."

"The relationship had taught me to care more about fidelity, although I'm still not convinced that my husband subscribes to that theory. Yet we came back to one another afterwards, emotionally and physically. However, when problems recur in the marriage, I fantasize that another man will come and save me.

I'm just not actively looking at present, sort of the 'devil-you-know-won't-hurt-you' view of men. There are just too many men out there with problems. Why begin with another so fast? What bothers me most of all about the episode with my lover is that it destroyed the friendship he and I shared. I really valued the friendship more than the physical aspect which destroyed it. And in some ways he appealed to me more than my husband and that was difficult to let go of.

"So many of my friends have conducted these affairs and have ended up changing their lives as a result. This did not happen in my situation, but I learned a great deal about myself and it was important for me to live it. I remember confiding in a close friend and she absolutely cheered me on. She was in a bad marriage and conducting her own affair. I was instrumental in organizing her way out of her marriage, ironically. So although I put my experience behind me, I understood how powerful a romance with a lover can become and why. That was something I might not have understood had I not been involved myself."

Amanda's case is complex and interesting. Her involvement with men exists on multiple levels and seems introspective and thoughtful. She is consumed with developing a full, rewarding relationship with a man. Her aspiration is to live in a particular way with a man, a search perhaps for equality and friendship. She is not content in a marginal marriage and for that reason she has suffered.

Her tryst with her lover was disappointing because, like her husband, he also fell short of her fantasy.

Amanda's search is not a desperate one but rather a personal struggle to connect positively with a man. She is somewhat unique in that she still sets high expectations for the marriage. She sought another man out of her frustration. She does not suffer from low self-esteem as we have witnessed in some other situations.

CR&O

Rita

Rita is forty years old and from Pasadena, California, where she lives presently. She grew up in a matriarchal family, a Catholic home with traditional values. She was raised by her grandmother and mother. After high school she became a flight attendant. It was then that she met her husband, a Vietnam vet with a drug addiction she was unaware of. She describes her marriage as a form of prison. By the time she was twenty-three she had a baby.

"After that I periodically left my husband to stay at my mother's with the baby. When I was close to thirty I met Dennis, who became my lover and remains so today. Eventually I got divorced and went back to school to begin a degree in guidance counseling. I had been through so much alone. There was Dennis, who provided support. He is ten years older, white and educated. I was curious about him; it seemed like the right move at the time. He was willing to take care of me and pay attention to my son. At first that seemed important and we had a relationship for many years that worked. But he has disappointed me and his lack of interest in life is discouraging."

Two years ago Rita developed cancer and had a hysterectomy. At that stage Dennis became detached.

"My mother had just died of cancer and I was frightened by it. He said we could no longer have sex because he was concerned about catching it. It was irrational and he is not stupid, so I assumed it was a selfish act on his part. I have remained with him because I need the financial support. For me, these men are about convenience. Not sex and not love. But I was very low after the surgery and I needed affirmation of my womanhood. That was when I met a coworker. The rejection by Dennis was awful. I had to be appreciated by someone else."

Although Rita is not ready to leave Dennis, and remains connected, she has taken on a new lover.

"This was someone I thought would help me. We work together and I definitely pursued him. I was bored with Dennis and ready for some excitement. I purposely chose this man because I thought it would be in my favor. He is a young white man and has a powerful position in the company. That appealed to me. I wanted to share his status, in a sense. I felt that he could provide me with things that counted. After a while Dennis chose not to do so. I felt cheated. My lover offered security in terms of my job—a raise, a car—with the expectation that I would work hard and be motivated. But from the start it was dangerous, a mixed bag. I never got the car. Instead he gave me a watch so I would get to work on time."

The affair took place at work, and Rita tells us it was conducted on a daily basis for a long stretch of time.

"For months we had sex in the back office. I never knew if it was really happening or if it was a fantasy, it was so muddled. Eventually I wanted out of any emotional/sexual connection and he wasn't ready to accept that."

Ultimately, Rita's bitterness and lack of trust toward men persists.

"All men are assholes. My dildo is more interesting than any lover I've ever had. Men are jerks, limited, unpleasant beings at best. I've always preferred white men. Not that I'm happy with this choice. I'd rather have a love relationship that works. But it hasn't happened. The lovers I've taken on, Dennis and the young man at work, have let me down. I do not wish to pursue any other man at this stage. If I say a relationship is over, as I did with Dennis and with my lover at work, neither of them believes me. There is no love here, just a power play on their part. I want to finish my degree, which is the only thing that makes me feel worthwhile."

Both men still play a prominent role in Rita's life. Dennis has refused to move out and the affair at work has "cooled off" but is not over.

"Men are secondary. I wish both of these men would disappear. I saw them only as vehicles to help me get ahead. I have purposely chosen two white lovers and a white husband hoping that for me, an uneducated Hispanic woman, they would be my meal ticket out. They have to understand that I don't care for them emotionally. It's perverse—they actually seem turned on by my attitude. I know now that I could not depend on any man. The key to freedom for me is being educated, and I am achieving this."

Rita perceived herself as imprisoned by her marriage. She broke out by taking on a relationship with a man. The lover provided an escape from her circumstances and allowed her to move out of a destructive situation. For Rita, the hope remains that with her next lover she will finally be able to develop a love relationship that is satisfying.

CRBO

Anna

Anna is forty years old and lives in a city in Virginia. She describes her childhood as "wonderful" and her marriage of twenty years as presently unhappy. Anna proceeds to tell us about her relationship with her lover.

"I have four children and was married by the time I was twenty years old. I'd say that for the last ten years marriage has not been solid, and finally, several years ago, I began to look toward other men. I consider myself a woman's woman but I was never someone who stayed by my husband's side or a woman friend's side at a big party. I've always gravitated toward men. I've always wanted to explore."

What Anna feels began as "a flirtation and good clean fun" became an extramarital relationship two years ago.

"I had never gotten involved with other men. It wasn't my interest or my inclination. This man is my husband's good friend and there I was, attracted to him. We lived in the same town and knew all the same people. So at first we'd simply go to lunch, see each other out in the open. He'd call on my birthday, send me flowers. I enjoyed his company always, even when we went out as couples. Finally lunch led to a movie and dinner when my husband was out of town. I'd look forward to these dates."

Anna felt the situation was complicated by the fact that she and her lover's wife were close friends.

"His wife never knew anything about it, although I'm beginning to wonder if she's suspicious now. And she's so socially connected, they both are, that it's been kept a very deep secret. In our circle of friends, this couple is considered to have the 'perfect' marriage."

While Anna tells us that she was surprised by the turn the relationship took, from friendship to extramarital affair, her lover said that he "always expected it to happen."

"We went to hotels together, traveling hours in order to avoid getting caught. We met regularly twice a week. At first it seemed to me to be a fantasy, as if it wasn't really happening as it unfolded. Then the sex part took over, changing everything. And while the sex is good, it isn't great. I never entered the relationship for sex. My sex life at home was never the issue. I just find that with this man I end up having more sex. We do it more frequently than I do it with my husband. And it is another level of intimacy."

At first Anna did not experience any strain upon the marriage as a result of her relationship with the other partner. But eventually she suffered from guilt.

"I think the catalyst for the guilt was the physical aspect of the affair. Initially, when we were meeting for lunch and it was all a kind of game, I saw it as a healthy ego boost. Once I was sleeping with two men at once, it became very stressful. And seeing this couple socially has become awkward.

"My lover is the most esteemed man in town, a gentle, kind, respected man. When I'm with him I feel beautiful, sexy, happy and yet vulnerable. Maybe I don't believe it's a natural thing to have this relationship going on. Perhaps that's why I suffer the guilt."

Anna and her lover have discussed the idea of breaking off the relationship and both agree it would be for the best, yet they are unable to do so.

"I'm not a risk taker and it's frustrating to feel I'm in a risky situation. Neither of us would give up our social lives or our families for the affair we have, so it isn't a love affair, but an attraction. In other words, we question how great our commitment to each other is if neither of us is willing to give up anything. We're very balanced this way, but it seems foolish to be so pragmatic and be in the midst of an affair."

The reason that Anna cannot let go of the connection with her lover is because she feels that she and her husband do not communicate.

"My husband and I got married very young. I knew very little about men but as long as the marriage was strong it didn't seem to matter. Once we had children and the communication between us began to break down, I found myself drawn physically to someone else. I never thought he was as handsome as my husband although I like his physique. I found the difference between my lover and my husband interesting. I liked the fact that he was not a native Virginian, that he came from a background so unlike mine. While I wouldn't have chosen it in a marriage, I like it in this setting. I kept thinking that his background made him into the kind of man he is, so much more willing to listen to me, to be there for me."

Anna hopes to end the situation despite her attachment to her other partner.

"I think about him all the time. Sometimes I know I should stop.

In fact, I consider us in a slowdown phase right now. The choice I'd make is to remain married, if had to make a choice. On the other hand, my goal throughout has been to strengthen the marriage, and in a strange way I feel that this relationship has done that. I understand what I have and what I don't have better than I understood it before. If I become stronger, I'll be able to say no altogether. I wonder that I'm so grateful to him for the experience, for the fire he puts under me. I feel like he's shown me emotions I didn't know I had: jealousy, a sense of self, a dedication to my marriage even as I conducted an affair."

The confusion for Anna sets in when she "lives two lives." While she explains that she realizes how and why women have lovers, she also recognizes the danger in the experience.

"I will never do this again but I'm not sorry that it started. The entire episode enriched my life. I do understand why a woman, especially today, seeks out another layer of her life. I imagine myself as married in any age but capable of going beyond it in some way. And that is what I have done."

It sounds as if Anna is rationalizing her situation as opposed to understanding what is really going on. Because she was discontented with the marriage she sought a relationship outside of it. She was at a needy point in her life and she desperately hoped and wanted to escape. Part of the attention she desired had to do with this need. To avoid the unhappiness she felt within the marriage she chose an affair. She wished to avoid not only the marriage but also her entire family life. She was not sensing a connection, which is why she moved away from it.

However, pragmatism rules the day, and it seems as if she is forcing herself to end the affair rather than staying with it to its natural conclusion.

CR80

Susan

Susan, the oldest of several children, lives in Georgia. She was married at twenty-four to a man five years older and has been married for fifteen years, although she and her husband lived together before they were married. Susan's childhood was "ordinary," she says, and her parents' marriage was solid. Since her children were small she has worked in the real-estate business.

Susan considers her marriage today to be better than in the past, but "lacking" in certain areas. Along the way, she conducted several extramarital relationships.

"The major affair occurred at a business convention. I had been married for ten years at the time. It was not my first affair, but the longest-standing one. It lasted three years and my husband did find out at the end. My lover was married also. We lived in different cities and it was a long-distance relationship. I saw him monthly for the most part, but it varied, sometimes more, sometimes less.

"I was not attracted to him physically but to his niceness. We were in the same business and he gave me ideas and paid a lot of attention to me. We'd talk for hours on the phone. My husband had little time for me. He was into his own thing and I was into mine. Our children had no part in my affairs. They always came first; what happened to me had nothing to do with my children. I always felt that way.

"It didn't bother me that I was sleeping with two men at once. One had no connection to the other. My lover and I met in totally different places. I'd fly up to meet him and he'd fly down to meet me. We'd stay at a hotel and it was fabulous. It was great to be together, like being on vacation."

In this situation, Susan found that sex was "never" her motivation. Her sexual relations with her husband were "equally good."

"I wanted the attention. I wanted to hear that I looked good, that I did a good job at work. He made me feel good and he made me laugh. That he was not my type physically and that my husband is better looking and more successful and in better physical condition was kind of weird. Still, I wanted to be with this man; I wanted the affair. He took care of me, he paid for our incredible long-distance phone bill and got me my own calling card. And part of the juggling act in order to see him was covered by my family. They knew, and while they said they couldn't understand, they covered for me anyway, giving me the room I needed to keep the relationship going."

The affair stopped when Susan's lover's wife discovered the romance. She confronted Susan and it was at this juncture that Susan felt she needed to tell her husband the situation.

"His wife was like a detective and began to pressure him. They had no children and she made it her business to learn about the affair. I told my husband before she told him. I wanted to be the one to tell him. He wasn't bad about it, because by then the affair was really over and his attitude was that he didn't own me. Meanwhile, this man's wife flew down to meet me and we went to an airport hotel to talk. We sat and talked for two hours about how she could keep her husband happy. I had met her before at a conference, but this was crazy, this meeting. Especially because I would have left my husband for him, but he never thought he could support me the way I wanted. His wife was the breadwinner and he couldn't justify my lifestyle. In a way I didn't want to leave my husband. I'd been juggling things quite well. I always looked at these affairs as separate from my marriage. But this affair was the big one."

Susan believes that her marriage improved with each affair that she experienced.

"It was as if my husband realized that other men were out there who would be attracted to me and that caused him to act better. That lasted a little while and then he'd stop paying attention again and I'd meet someone new. It wasn't as if I was looking for someone. It seemed to happen. There was one affair in particular that caused a lot of trouble. It took place in my hometown.

"We were best friends with another couple and living in Memphis at the time. Our kids were friends, in a playgroup together. His wife and I were best friends. He and I got together. I don't know exactly how it became that way. We were seen together and it was no big deal because everyone knew that we were all friendly. The four of us would go out for dinner and he'd sort of play with me under the table. After one month, it became an affair. Then we rented a beach house together and it was fine, except for one incident that turned everything around.

"He and I made a truce that we wouldn't fool around at the rental house. It was too close with our spouses and the children. It was his birthday and we planned a surprise party. Evidently someone who came to the party knew or suspected and told this guy's wife. She flipped out. They've since divorced, but the night it happened, that was the end. There was a big scene and I told him to take her home or I'd tell everything. We've never spoken since. My husband was hurt because he and the man were such close friends. It had only lasted six months and I hadn't been emotionally involved. I actually felt it wasn't a big deal."

The most recent attachment caused a tremendous upset. When Susan's husband was transferred for work, Susan remained behind to sell the house. It was the affair that occured during this interval that was the "turning point" for her.

"My husband moved quickly and began his new job. I became friendly with a divorced father while my husband was away. My husband rarely came home and I went to dinner with this guy all the time. He was the first lover I'd had who wasn't married and had so much freedom, as I did. I assumed that my husband was having affairs by then, but I thought it was for the sex and not for any kind of relationship, so I did not feel threatened.

"There I was with a man who seemed to be the last person I'd pick for an affair. I don't know what I saw in him. I liked how he treated me but he wasn't attractive at all. One night I decided to try him. We became very close after that; he fell head over heels for me. It was great fun for him but it wasn't like the lover I'd had for so many years. Nothing was like that. I think the fact that I was married, the danger of it, made the sex exciting for this one. But he wasn't the best sexually by any means. He said he wanted to marry me and asked me not to move.

"Finally I had sold our house and was waiting for the movers to come. My husband still wasn't around but I expected him the week of the move. It came down to the wire with my lover begging me to stay and my husband coming home to get me. When the movers and my husband arrived, I decided not to go. I told my husband I wanted a divorce, that I'd found someone else. I actually stayed and got divorced. I lived with this lover for six weeks, and he had kids from hell and an ex-wife who was loony.

"I moved out. I saw that I didn't want to be divorced unless I was doing it to get remarried. I didn't want to be alone. It was horrible. Then, three months later, my ex-husband found someone. Financially I was in bad shape. I decided I'd better move to the Northeast, where my family is. If you can believe what happened, I saw my ex-husband when he came to pick up the kids and we got reunited. He said he wanted me back. So I remarried him."

Today, Susan tells us, she is fairly certain that she would not conduct an affair.

"I'm not sorry I had them and I didn't feel guilty. I can't say I'll never have them. My husband has changed enough that he's filling the voids now. The affairs were never for sex but for the emotional parts that were missing. Today I am more settled in my marriage."

Susan's story is one in which she relies heavily on denial as a defense against anxiety and guilt. Her multiple involvements with men are the reason she feels so anxious and guilt-ridden in the first place.

The sexuality is interesting in that Susan does not appear especially motivated by it. Rather, she has sexualized her emotional needs without realizing it. She also lacks the ability to anticipate the consequences of her own actions. As a result she gets into real difficulty, psychologically and practically speaking.

One wonders about Susan's superego and whether it is underdeveloped. The meaningful question is, why would it be? Perhaps there is something in her background that explains her needs and her behavior.

ରେ৪০

Tiana

Tiana is forty-two years old and lives in Florida, where she grew up. Graduating from high school at sixteen, she married the same year. Because her parents signed for her to marry, Tiana had the feeling that they "wanted her gone."

Tiana explains that she never felt wanted, having been adopted by a minister and his wife. She grew up as "a pretty, blonde little girl," while the family was "dark and average." The minister and his wife had two children and Tiana never fit in.

"I married early to get away. I thought I was making them happy and doing something for myself. I was so naive it was incredible. My husband was thirty-two when I was sixteen. Twice my age at the time. Imagine it! He'd been married two times already. The saving grace was that I looked twenty-four. He was in the service and I'd been going to the club with my girlfriends. That was how we met. He was very neat and handsome. So I married him."

While her husband was overseas, Tiana decided to get a college degree.

"I was in college while my good friends continued to fool around with the guys at the base. I was extremely pretty. [Guys in] cars would stop downtown to stare at me when I was that young. I felt aware of myself and it was difficult. I knew that men were attracted to me. I was very shy. I tried to hide my figure because I felt men wanted me for my body. I wanted someone to want me for me. My family upbringing was so strict that I was in constant battle with what I'd been taught and the way my life was going. My husband returned and he was the one who exploited me.

"My husband decided I'd be a good belly dancer. It was strange that he would position me like that, but as I said, I was very young. He was the one who put me into the clubs. His friends ran the club near the base. He had me dance there and I did so well he took me to Miami. I was known as his wife who danced but whenever he was away, the other officers would call and ask me out. If my husband was aboard ship, I was called, all the time."

Tiana did not respond to the attention she received when she first married.

"I was careful and inexperienced. I had no idea of the life my husband led. When he was home we had a home on the water in Florida and we lived on a different level than how I live today. Today I am with my lover of many years and it is not what I expected it to be. It took me a long time to respond to another man and I cannot believe my choice or how my life has turned out.

"I met Tom through my husband. He was in show business and my husband booked me at his club. He was attracted to me from the beginning. I remember the first night that I performed. He grabbed me at the end of the night, when he was to pay me. I was very aware of his intentions but I was careful back then. I kept thinking, he's not my type. But the physical attraction was always there. After a while we got involved. He had a lot of warmth and I was so drawn to him physically, it wouldn't go away. With my husband, sex was as if I was a mechanical toy. He was cold and would not show his feelings. That was why I wanted to be with Tom. I wanted to know how different it could be."

Tiana tells us that before she and her lover became involved, there were "signs" that he was difficult.

"Before we were living together, when we were first seeing one another, I'd bought a very expensive dress. He told me to take it off immediately. He told me it was too expensive and that I couldn't keep it. My husband wasn't like that. With him there were other problems. Tom was domineering and jealous. Not once did he help me financially, in all the years we've been together. The strong physical attraction is what held up. Today I feel trapped. While I was afraid to leave my husband for financial reasons, now I'm afraid to leave Tom but not willing to marry him for financial reasons."

For the first three years of Tiana's relationship with Tom, they did not live together.

"Only in the last five years have we shared a house. Once my husband died I knew that I had to go on with my life. I understood he wasn't coming back. So I stayed with Tom and at first it seemed safe, while now it seems disastrous. I learned too late that my husband had cheated, that he was a typical officer. He drank and smoked heavily and saw other women. He'd be gone for weeks at a time. I was so young at first and then too stupid to get it, to suspect. Then I saw him with a woman. That was it for me. I'd raised his children and I'd been true to him for years. I suppose the discovery pushed me toward Tom. I ended up raising Tom's children too. But it was worth it, because when I felt secure and safe, I was very happy.

"I would describe Tom as a lover as never exciting but very comfortable. He taught me so many things. I was really hooked on the sex. The sex that was so great is less so now. He has become heavy and less enticing. Day-to-day life is the problem. It doesn't work for us. He's too demanding and expects too much of me. He tells me how to wear my hair and how to dress. If he likes my style, he wants to change it anyway. He wants to be lord and master in everything.

I remember how attentive and different he was when I was married and I can't believe what has happened."

Tiana remains in the marriage because of fear, and because of her approach to men in general.

"If I didn't think all men were rotten, I'd go elsewhere. I meet men through my work in antiques and at art shows. I've had opportunities to be with other types of men, affluent, educated men. I stay with Tom, too numb to feel much for him. It certainly isn't the love affair it was. Loving someone isn't enough if he's lost your money and bosses you around, especially if it started as sexual and as an escape.

"My hope is that I can afford to build a life for myself. I do not feel I am my own person and yet I'm not totally unhappy. The parts of the relationship that work confuse me. I assume Tom has some need to push me around and I try to be tolerant. As one gets older, one thinks, well, everyone else has someone, so I guess I have to also. That's how Tom became my live-in from being someone who saw me on occasion and lavished attention upon me.

"After the hurt from my husband and then from Tom, my lover, I know I could be happy alone. I feel trapped enough to take Prozac to get me through some days. My strict upbringing haunts me throughout. When other men ask me out, and it still happens, I dare not do it. I live with Tom; that's a commitment I have to see to an end. Until I leave for another, it feels like a marriage to me."

Tiana felt rejected by her parents and experienced herself as a burden. She fell into this early marriage in an effort to release her parents and also get rid of the feeling of being unwanted. Unfortunately, she was used by her husband. She rebelled, in a sense, and became involved with another man who was equally destructive. Tiana has been involved in seriously problematic relationships with men and appears unable to break free of this pattern.

CR80

Tess

Tess, at the age of forty-four, feels that her connection with her lovers has involved both positive and negative episodes. Twice married, Tess grew up an only child in a small town in the Northeast. Her parents divorced when she was eleven and she remained with her mother. She was first married at the age of twenty-two, a marriage which lasted four years, a "flat, unemotional, unpleasant marriage."

When asked why she married this man, Tess replied, "He was a good salesman; he sold himself. He was successful, with good looks, from a good family. He made me an offer I couldn't refuse." She admitted that from the time she got married to her first husband, she "always looked at other men" and was not faithful. The lovers varied.

"Oh, God, I was so young. Some were good, some weren't. We met at wonderful restaurants and at elegant clubs. It was the excitement and the intensity of being together that created the high. It wasn't for the sex; I wasn't sex-oriented. I have friends, women friends, who would disagree. I mean, they have lovers and go to these sleazy hotels with them near the tunnel. They become obsessed with the men, buying fancy expensive underwear and getting all made up, their hair, a manicure, for these dates. They don't seem one bit worried about their husbands finding out or noticing a difference in their behavior. And one guy, my friend's lover, he goes to sex shops and surprises her. Now I was never into that but it's around, it happens. I only wanted lovemaking and romance. I didn't do it for escape but to create a new reality, to prepare myself for a life without my spouse. I never thought of these relationships as noncommittal. There were so many and always I was looking for a real relationship, one that mattered. And I always found one."

Ironically this was not how she met her second husband. In her search for the other partner to share time with, a search for love fulfillment, none of those lovers won out. She described them as everything from Club Med G-O's to a lawyer at a white-shoe firm. Tess says these lovers were adventurous and exciting.

"You know, it's funny. I had no fears of being caught. I would have cared if I had been caught, but I didn't feel like it mattered. Once I actually went to Paris with my lover while my husband was away on a business trip and he didn't even know. I was twenty-six years old. At the time I loved that person. It was a very short-lived relationship. He was extremely attractive.

"But the one who really destroyed me was the lawyer. I would have married him if he'd asked me to. And I would have been sorry later."

Tess explains that she decided to get divorced because she wanted to be with someone else. She had no one specific in mind at the time that she sought a divorce, but was determined that her future would be with a partner.

"I never wanted to be alone. I was looking for the next relationship but not for a husband." However, within three months of her divorce, she was married again.

In her second marriage, she did not look for a lover as she had in the first. There was only one extramarital relationship, which occurred a month before the marriage ended. Tess described this lover as "another type."

"Someone very different from my husband in every way—in looks, background, style. I had a real need for change. As if I traveled from here to there and then I backtracked in both marriages. Everyone has a light side and a dark side and that part of me, the dark side, wasn't developed. I kept exploring the possibilities. The first person that I married was the same type as the last person I cheated with. So, in fact, I began and finished at the same place. It closed the cycle.

"You see, for me, feeling young and feeling free are two separate things. These relationships I had were new, and I was free. They offered act one, act two and act three. The newness is the most stimulating part of the game for me. The game of finding out about a new person, someone to listen to, to think about. Not act three, the sex part—that's the least of it.

"Watching the evolution of the relationship is what I like, watching them get turned on by you. The sex is overrated. The turn-on is the first kiss, the first touch. I'm highly sensual, not sexual. Although one of my husbands is an amazing lover, it wasn't a turn-on for me. In fact, he was so good there was nothing for me to do."

The ages of Tess's lovers were never an issue. Most of the men were near her own age at the time, although there was one who was ten years younger and one who was fifteen years younger. She explains her present state of mind:

"After a while it's all the same. All men are predictable. They have to be exceptional to be anything else. If academically better prepared than me, it's a plus, but as far as introspection, perception, they haven't got a clue."

She feels she paid an "exorbitant price in terms of energy and time" in her relationships with her other partners.

"I am smack in the middle of it while it is going on. I'm not on the outside looking in. I'm right there. But ultimately it exhausts you. The time I spent thinking about them. Not the sex but fantasies of when we'd be together again, organizing meetings. Even without kids. Imagine. It does exhaust you. It's like a cheating of the mind."

Tess's search for a multiple reality is quite fascinating. There are women who realize this at some period in their lives. For those who recognize it, it is the requirement that pushes them toward a lover and out of a traditional love relationship. For Tess it sounds more like an escape from reality.

CB80

Vivien

Vivien is fifty years old and lives in a metropolitan area. After twenty-five years of marriage, she has recently divorced. She has children and was "comfortable" with her marriage for many years.

"I thought the marriage was okay, although something was always missing. I think I stayed basically because I felt obliged to raise the children and life wasn't that bad. I guess one gets into a routine and figures that this is what life is.

"I always wondered what was out there, though I didn't act on it for fifteen years. Then I had my first affair. This happened when I was in my late thirties. I felt it was time to move on. I was away and I met a man who was a foreigner. We met in a nonthreatening environment, which made it easier. I suddenly felt terrific and really alive. But he lived abroad, so I wasn't able to see him again. And the attraction had been only physical. I look at this affair as the first break from the mold."

The next encounter for Vivien occurred soon after, and became more of a commitment.

"This man lived closer to home. He wasn't married but he lived with someone. He was more my age than my husband was, more of a peer. He was very persistent and asked me to meet him for a drink, for dinner, constantly. Because he was from out of town, we'd go back to his hotel and have great sex. I didn't really care about him but it was great sex. He was an incredible lover. I think the sex was always the thing. We became attached to each other based on this amazing physical relationship that we shared. The situation lasted a long time.

"I'd see him at least two times a month but we spoke often on the phone and at some point I either pretended or thought I cared. In other words, I got involved but I knew I didn't love him. It became an obsession anyway. If I didn't have him, how would I get through, how could I get by? I clung to the relationship. In a way it prolonged my marriage. It was my secret life that gave me a reason to exist."

Vivien tells us that she experienced no guilt as a result of her relationship. Her life felt richer for having "two lives."

"My husband wasn't so interested in sex so it wasn't a big deal to sleep with another man. I would see him as much as I could. I was very involved."

Then, through work, Vivien met someone else.

"Because of my work schedule I saw many people separately from the marriage. I'd go out and meet people, a wider range. One of the people I met I began to fall for. I started having an affair with him too. I carried on two affairs while I was married for a period of time. He was single and available, having just gotten divorced. I began to see him and we spoke a lot about who I was and the situation I was in. He wondered why I'd lead a double life. My kids were older by then. He helped me realize that I could go, that I could leave the marriage and give up my other affair.

"I was afraid to leave a long-term marriage, though. I'd never been alone. I was in my forties and I decided to get divorced. Although I'm happy not to be married, I'm now financially devastated. That's the only part that I miss. It's amazing to think I lived with someone for so long and that I never look back at the marriage. Never."

Today Vivien remains in a relationship with her last lover.

"I do not want to be married again. Although a serious commitment is fine, there's a freshness to being tied to someone without having to be married. There's no role-playing if it's not a marriage, simply a relationship. As much as I need money, I don't think that marrying someone for money is for me. Instead, I'm looking for work that is fulfilling.

"In looking back on the two relationships outside my marriage, I suppose they motivated me to do something, to act, to move forward. I know that being in therapy didn't help me at all. These men were the catalyst for me. I didn't leave my husband for either man, but they got me into gear. Then I left for myself."

Vivien has heavy sexual needs. She definitely remained in the marriage as a security operation.

Her affairs seemed like emotional journeys that were necessary to her growth. Two affairs plus a marriage is quite an undertaking. Yet Vivien's needs were such that she walked through these relationships.

ϓϒ

Camille

Camille, separated at thirty-nine, describes her new status as "being set free." She lives in southern California, has left a husband of fifteen years and is living alone with her child. Growing up in the Southwest, her childhood was "intact and happy." Coming from a traditional family, Camille had strong feelings about marriage and family. Her recent decision has had a tremendous impact on her life.

"I think that the kind of family I came from had a great deal to do with how difficult it was for me to leave my husband and break up my own family. So in retrospect I'm not surprised to find myself one of these women who leaves her husband and examines the fabric of her life. I didn't anticipate it until it was upon me. I wonder if it was inevitable or might I have never left it if I hadn't met my lover?"

Camille tells us that she married her "best friend" from college, after many ups and downs in the relationship. While it was never sexual or passionate, her husband was considered a "great catch" and she thought they worked well together.

"I left my husband once in my twenties and then again, now that

I'm in my late thirties. Both times it was a reaction to who he had become. As a medical-school student he paid the price of giving up his life to medicine, and then as a doctor he paid the price of being treated like a god all day and unable to function at home, in reality. When I first left him it was because I wanted to have fun and feel alive, and when I met my lover, it was for the same reason. I've never changed, I've always been who I am."

Nine years ago, when their child was born, Camille began to feel smothered. Giving up a career and autonomy, moving from a city to a small town, she rebelled at the concept of becoming a housewife.

"I might have compromised for the sake of my child, but I was never a good wife that way, a housewife, and I never promised to be. I'm also well educated and ambitious and this was killing me. I suppose that had I remained in the city as a young mother it might have worked. But the combination of living in a small town, with motherhood upon me, became too much. My career opportunities were limited. Where I live has impacted everything that was to follow."

What Camille describes as a "classic" response to her "drama" was the meeting of her lover.

"I felt very alone even in my perfect life. I was a doctor's wife, well respected in the community, with a lovely home and sweet child. I convinced myself it was so perfect that I couldn't admit for ages that something was wrong with me, something that I wanted to fix. My husband had little time for my life. His practice grew and flourished and we had less and less communication. He had no heartfelt interest in me or my life and never heard what I had to say. Eventually I found other interests, art, ceramics, my child's school. Then we remodeled the house.

"It really began two years ago with the house. I gave it all my energy; it was demanding timewise and energywise. I was rewarded by the outcome. The work was impressive and I began to remember my talents and strengths. I put my heart and soul into that house.

And when I think of it today, I think of the doorknobs. There were these very expensive doorknobs that I felt were necessary. My husband was tired of writing checks and only grudgingly noticed the results. Not that he didn't want this house—he did. The doorknobs symbolize the money spent and my husband's lack of understanding. It did something to me, his reaction to the goddamn doorknobs. I was out there, finally being creative, living to my potential, and he could only complain about doorknobs. I was trapped."

At this time, Camille began her liaison with her lover.

"Last summer I started a relationship with another man. We'd known each other and then met again socially. He was also married at the time. At first it was a friendship, then it became an affair. He was so different from my husband, both professionally and in background. That was absolutely part of the attraction initially. Both of us in the early stages considered it a fling. I'd had one before this, so I understood what it meant. But I really liked him from the start. He brought out the creative, fun side of me, the wacky aspect, a part of me that had been lost for so long, taken over by the role of a doctor's wife, a mother, an outstanding citizen in a conservative town not unlike the southern town where I grew up. I understood what it meant to be aberrant in this atmosphere, and in the beginning days of the affair, we were careful. I was conscious of violating a trust. But my husband didn't even notice the flowers my lover sent. My needs were not met in the marriage."

Camille views her lover as the catalyst, not the cause, of the separation that followed.

"The relationship awakened me, not creating a new me but reviving the lost me. I expected it to strengthen the marriage with positive energy. My lover is a fellow artist and a true friend. I told myself I'd never leave my husband because my feelings for someone I'd spent my entire adulthood with, the father of my child, can't evaporate. And I still love him today. I can't just slam the door on those major feelings. I had trouble separating the feelings of love from the feeling of guilt."

Camille describes her time spent with her lover as "passionate."

"At first the relationship was compartmentalized. I was able to handle both. My lover enhanced me so I enhanced the marriage. What my husband couldn't provide my lover could. I became complete. It wasn't only sexual but sex played a big part in it. We are the same age, have children the same age, and managed to see one another only during the week. We'd make arrangements—one of us would find someone's home or we'd go to his office to be alone. We never went to a hotel. It was shocking for both of us that we'd actually fallen in love with each other. I can't separate the sex from the rest but I think one of the reasons it's so wonderful is because the relationship is so wonderful. The newness and electricity of it is certainly not like twenty years with the same man.

"My lover really listens to me. All our concerns were shared and paid attention to and it spills over into the sex. With someone tuned into me, it's a remarkable difference."

When asked if she became obsessed with the affair, Camille tells us that she did and that her lover did as well. As a result of the obsession, they became careless and the affair was discovered.

"Maybe we wanted it to happen, who knows? We only knew we were in love and frightened by that. I kept saying I wouldn't leave my family and he said he wasn't sure what he'd do. We agreed that whatever happened, we'd make our own decisions, not based on what the other chose. Intellectually it worked but emotionally it failed. Because my lover and I always expected to be together.

"After three or four months everything blew up because we were discovered. For our spouses' part, the ugliest emotions were unleashed—anger, hostility, jealousy, sorrow. It wasn't the way I wanted it to occur. I'm someone who likes to be in control and this was definitely out of control. It was painful for our spouses to be dragged through the mud for our sakes. I stood my ground, explaining to my husband that I wasn't leaving him for another man but for myself. I explained that it was a matter of priorities. I had decided, finally, that my priorities were to leave the 'ideal' life of a doctor's wife with the beautiful house and material comforts. I told him the relationship with my lover was inspirational, but not the answer. I realized that I could have more, that I deserve more than to feel half-dead. If I hadn't experienced this love, I would believe most love affairs are really only about sex. But I know how much more it is than that. Several women have come up to me and expressed how they feel—they express the camaraderie of those fortunate enough to have been touched as I've been.

"Other people, especially in our small town, judge me and think I'm awful. But I've followed my heart versus my intellect and I'm hoping my intellect will follow. I felt strong and free, but it's a lonely decision. One is alone out there after all the years of protection once you make a choice like mine."

Today Camille has left her husband and continues to see her lover.

"I'm living my life day to day, with the breathing room I need. I've moved into a rental apartment and am not living with my lover. I still need a sense of self I never want to lose it again. I need to figure out what I want for the second half of my life, having no regrets about the first half. I'm not rushing into anything. Certain days I wake up feeling wonderful and other days I can't believe what I've done. But I've become very brave."

Camille waits for her divorce and her lover waits for his. They are still together, still "very much in love," and the community has calmed down in its reactions to this event. She believes that "out of the confusion will come a certainty and clarity" that she welcomes.

In contrast to certain interviewees, Camille truly suffered with her affair. It was not easy for her to merely be intimate sexually. Having viewed herself as the "perfect wife," the break from this role was particularly painful. She had a strong identity as mother and wife but she struggled with it, questioning its importance.

Camille is unusual in several ways. She did not use the romance to get out of her marriage, although it provoked her departure. Once she became immersed with her lover, the affair took over. She left her husband in the wake of the affair, but the affair was only the impetus, not the reason. The affair was part of a personal, emotional journey for Camille, which is not always the case with women and their lovers.

ᘔᘓ

Piaffe

Having lived in Kentucky most of her life, Piaffe portrays herself as someone attached to a place. Her childhood was "extremely low-key and pleasant." In her mid-thirties today, she was married at the age of twenty-five to a man she had lived with for four years. The marriage lasted for five years, and during that time she had several encounters with other partners.

Piaffe's marriage was happy in the early stages. Only after they began to "run in the fast lane" did she see it deteriorate.

"I think it was a combination of our lifestyle and my husband's being in medical school that first forced a wedge between us. I worked at a lab and I was constantly exposed to chemical abuse. He was in medical school and had similar exposure. At the same time, we were meeting people at work and in school who were involved with drugs. One thing led to another. I suppose I began first; I began to have affairs."

The stepping-off point for Piaffe was that first lover, "the most romantic man" she'd ever met.

"The first was the most difficult, as if you're on a diet and you go for that first spoon of ice cream. After the first spoonful, it's okay, once you've begun. The rules are already broken, you might as well keep going. Then the affairs became fair game; the sanctity of my marriage had been destroyed and somehow it no longer mattered to me how many men I had outside the marriage.

"I was visiting some friends and they introduced us. My husband never learned about this particular affair. I think of it as a relationship about fulfilling dreams not fulfilled by my marriage. This lover was terrific, a dreamy kind of man. I'd never met anyone so exciting and charming. He was foreign and alluring. I was caught up in the entire episode, not one isolated layer, like sex or romance. I saw him several times and each time it had that heat. That never went away. But we lived far from each other and eventually it died out."

The next attachment to another partner took place in Piaffe's hometown. The man was unmarried and the relationship lasted for almost two years.

"Finally I left him because he had a problem with alcohol and it colored everything. I was suffering with my own trouble with drugs and the combination was lethal. Yet this man showed me how poor a marriage I had. It really began to dawn on me as a result of a connection to another man that my husband and I came from such different places—our family origins and issues around it which remained unresolved—that we couldn't be together. Because my marriage had this slick, prevalent style, using drugs, running with a fast crowd, it was hard to see the forest for the trees. My second lover helped me. His alcohol addiction made me realize my own addiction. I began to get in touch with my own feelings. I understood that if I didn't give up drugs and give up my marriage, I'd lose me."

Yet Piaffe did not leave her marriage immediately. One more relationship developed before she made her move.

"I fell in love with a married man. This was a situation that lasted for over a year. During that time I saw him several times a week because my husband was on call by then, and in the hospital constantly. The affair was a rich attachment, on many levels. There was intimacy, great, frequent sex, companionship, a sharing of thoughts and feelings. I had an all-encompassing relationship with someone who had a wife and kids I knew he'd never leave. I never even entertained the thought because I understood from the start that it wasn't a possibility. I loved him because he brought me what I lacked in my marriage– caring and nurturing."

Piaffe's time with this partner was spent at her house.

"We'd meet there once a week and always we had sex, although I can't say the relationship was predominantly sexual. I knew I'd never have children and I knew how important his children were to him. So we never talked about that, but we often discussed my leaving my husband and he was helpful in that way. He didn't encourage me, but in talking to him I realized I finally had to make my break.

"What I decided to do was to leave my husband and to stop having affairs. Although I have no regrets about these men, I knew the time had come to quit. One of the most difficult things for me had been sleeping with these men at the same time I slept with my husband. I had to drink in order to get into bed at night and I hated that. The pain in the marriage wouldn't go away no matter what I tried. So what I did was liberating and difficult at the same time."

In looking back on her attachments to other men, Piaffe tells us that they were "the fabric of my life and a learning experience."

"The lovers came out of an unhappiness but they showed me the way. I was taught about myself through these men. I'm very grateful for the chance to have given up drugs and to have left a sad, disappointing marriage."

Today Piaffe is living with a man and does not feel inclined to be married. Despite feeling her exposure to other men was "positive," she does not believe she'd take on a lover at this stage.

"I know now that I'd first work on a marriage or relationship before I'd go outside the boundaries in search of fulfillment. I think there are ways to heal and change without doing what I did."

Piaffe is an excellent example of a woman who has sought men outside the marriage as a way to help herself. By exploring other men she learned about herself. She became more mature and was able to make better decisions.

For Piaffe her lovers served as a vehicle, an honest vehicle in order to realize how to relate to a man. She became self-aware and self-confident so that she was able to leave her marriage and find a better situation. Her ability to articulate the difference between sexual and romantic ways of being with a man enabled her to negotiate her way through these attachments and move ahead.

0380

Jane

Jane is forty-two years old and lives in Minnesota. She is married and in the process of getting a divorce. The marriage was a working marriage for seven years and she and her husband have two children. Jane has been living with a man for the last year or so. She tells us that her childhood was "absolutely normal in every way" and that she always "expected to lead a similar existence."

"I was married at twenty-seven and had two kids by the time I was twenty-nine. The marriage was romantic at first, and I was in love with him in the beginning. But I always had male friends. In the beginning of the marriage, I made certain they were only friends. I was not looking at other men at that time.

"Once I had a baby I suspected that my husband was having an affair. I tried to sort things out because I wasn't sure it was the case. Then I confronted him and I said I was going to leave. In the end I decided to stay because we were going to Spain to live for his work.

I knew it would be an interesting experience and I had a business opportunity there. When I got to Spain I was upset. My husband was traveling often and I was saddled with the kids. We hired an au pair, a cute young guy, ten years younger than me.

"The au pair lived in our house. He was hired to take care of the kids, but when my husband would go on business trips during the week, it got to be more. I figured my marriage wasn't working and after a few months of the au pair being there, we were together. During the week it was fine but on the weekends it was difficult. We had to mask it. I wasn't guilty as I might have been if my marriage was good. I absolutely knew that my husband was fooling around."

Jane experienced "very good sex" with the au pair but it was the friendship which she believes drove the relationship.

"We are still very good friends today. He was younger and had no money. It was an odd situation. We were close and I loved him but I did not want to run off and marry him. For him I think it was a little scary. Seeing my husband and having to act normal was difficult for him. He felt a little guilty but I never did. Then he was a serious student and our relationship created problems for him. He questioned his life, what he wanted to do with it. I was sort of beyond that, for better or for worse. The children were too young to have any idea what was going on and my husband never knew."

The affair ended when Jane and her husband moved to another country.

"Then the intensity and the sexual part began to wane. It became more of a friendship once he no longer lived in our home. He came to visit sometimes, but it wasn't the same. I began to understand that the affair had occurred because I was lacking something in my marriage. If someone else fills the void, then that other relationship works for you. Also the physical attraction had been very strong. I'm not sorry that I had the tryst with the au pair. It carried me through a bad time. I happen to believe that affairs do make marriages bearable."

Becoming a mother was difficult for Jane, and she feels that that, and not the affair, was the actual catalyst for the end of the marriage.

"Having children brought out my husband's fear of responsibility. I couldn't give him the same attention I had before. Meantime he was rising on the corporate ladder. My being a mother and switching roles was too much for him to handle."

After the attachment to the au pair ended, Jane met the man she is living with today. By that time she had moved back to Minnesota.

"He is someone I met just as I was thinking of leaving my husband. For one year I still tried to see my husband and to make it work. I was also involved with this man, who was married at the time. I knew his wife too, and at first we were all friends. Then we began an affair. I'd see him during the day. We'd meet at my apartment. It was about sex and fun. He'd come over during the morning and we'd have this hot sex and passion. It wasn't like real life until we began to live together. At first we couldn't wait to jump in bed. The nice part was that we were the same age and old enough not to be inhibited. There weren't any holds on the relationship. There was a maturity.

"For me it was nice because I didn't have to commit myself and I didn't want to. It was nice for him because he'd been in a long, bad marriage. Then I began to fall for him. Eventually he made the decision to leave his marriage. Who knows if I was the catalyst to his leaving or not."

Jane fully intends to "make this relationship work."

"I don't think I'd go outside the relationship at this stage, although I came close, very close. Then I became frightened that my live-in was suspicious and I don't want to jeopardize this situation, having almost ruined it. I had met a man in my industry and I was physically attracted. Let's say I all but had an affair with him. Then

I realized that having an affair while you're married is different. Then the affair is an escape. But if you're not married, that escape isn't necessary. I don't want to stay and have an affair. Either I stay and I commit to it, or leave."

Jane is not sorry that she was involved with the au pair, or with the lover she now lives with.

"It carried me through a bad time. One has an affair because you're not willing to break up the marriage or for financial reasons or for the children. My circumstances today are different. While I'm always analyzing it, and I may no longer love him, it was a wild, passionate affair at the end of my marriage, when it began.

"I'm not one of those women who has to have a man all the time. I was always fiercely independent. And that proves a problem for most men. My little dalliances were nothing more, during the marriage. I really did not intend to give up the marriage but I felt forced to, because I wanted to forget the pain. I think the affairs made me see there was such pain in the marriage; they helped me find a way to leave. Not for the affairs but for myself."

Jane's story is typical in certain ways. She almost consciously used her lover to get out of her marriage. Again we see an affair being used as an escape from motherhood. It is also an interesting feature that her mothering seems to be difficult for her. The mothering was overwhelming and she looked to the affair as a way of being taken care of. The affair was a form of shelter.

There is a chance that Jane was secretly angry with her husband over his infidelity. There might be revenge at work here also.

CRWD

Randy

Married at twenty-two, Randy remained married for twenty years and is getting divorced today. From an "old Cape Cod" family, Randy tells us that her family is "nice and well schooled." Her husband comes from the same sort of background and they have two daughters.

"At the start of my marriage my husband put me on a pedestal. It was at a time when people were married at twenty. I think that I was married too young. I was a virgin when I married and in shock from the whole sex issue. What harmed the marriage, though, was gradual lack of communication both ways, between my husband and myself. After twenty years I knew there had to be more in life. Then I saw a man at work who I knew I wanted to be with. I knew it when I saw him. He was married also and together we began to meet as often as possible.

"I was definitely in love with my lover. The sex was terrific and I learned many things–things I'd never learned in twenty years of marriage. I was pulling away from my husband by then. I was nauseated to still sleep with him. But he was at work so often and for such long hours that my lover and I actually went to my apartment to have sex."

After a year with this lover, Randy was "destroyed" when he obtained a divorce from his wife and was "set free."

"He said he wanted to go out in the open and not sneak around. He wanted to be with women who were able to go places with him. I was crushed when he left me but I stayed married. The next thing I knew he was getting married again. That was when I decided I ought to leave my husband on the off chance that he'd leave his new wife for me. I hoped against hope. I knew, though, how he felt about stopping the affair and not wanting an illicit relationship. But because I was obsessed with him, and the attraction was beyond anything I'd ever known, I continually hoped that he'd leave his new wife."

The attraction to this lover, Randy believes, was "only about sex."

Nonetheless she was unable to let it go.

"I couldn't function, I was so crazy about him. After a while I realized I should stay in my marriage if I could stand it and simply take on another lover. This time I waited and thought carefully. I was determined not to be treated badly again. I was very flirtatious and sized men up, waiting for the right person. I saw my new lover as a friend first and a physical partner second. The affair began two years ago and is still going strong. While the sex and passion is not the same as with my first, this works well for me. I knew I used to glow in anticipation of seeing my first lover. It isn't like that this time, but there's a level of comfort I like.

"The marriage itself still had problems, which is why I felt forced to go somewhere else to begin with. My lover listens when I speak. The interaction with my husband never improved, not as a result of an affair or as a result of my wanting to leave the marriage. I felt the lovers were there for me, especially the second lover. My second lover is from a different culture. He is married and his wife had a baby during the affair, which made me very angry. He had promised that he no longer wanted to be in the marriage and the next thing I know, his wife is pregnant."

Randy views her affairs as having "crossed the line."

"Once I began, I was compelled to keep going. But I also realized that I wanted to get out of the marriage as a result of the affairs, the exposure to other men. I wanted a fulfilled life, not fulfilled moments here and there with a lover. These lovers showed me what was out there and I decided to leave a marriage that was not making me happy. Once my horrific divorce ends, I'll be on my way. Only recently, during my separation, did I decide I might want to leave my present lover. I've met someone else and I think it's time to move on. At last I'm getting to a place where I feel emotionally and physically gratified."

It is obvious that Randy begins her involvement with her lover as a compensatory move. She has to make up for her marriage at an early age. What is interesting, though, is that the compensatory nature of her relationship with her lover continues. What seems to be happening is that Randy has chosen to remain in a poor marriage while making up for it with her lovers.

We have no clear sense, from her story, of why she has decided on this route. The lovers become backup relationships as she waits for something better. It is as though Randy has split her emotional needs and directed a portion of these needs to one man, another portion to the other man.

CB80

Barbara

Barbara is forty-nine years old and lives in the Northeast. She was married at nineteen, a marriage that lasted for twenty years and produced two children. She explains her lifestyle and marriage as "something the outside world would admire," but inwardly she felt she was "suffering for a long time."

"When my husband and I were by ourselves, it was an inflammable, argumentative, verbally abusive situation. I remained true only because I looked around and decided that it wasn't that bad, there wasn't much out there that I was missing. I stayed for a long while with the two-car country-club life.

"Once I had an affair I realized what real love could be and that changed my life. I met my lover by accident at a train station. We went out for coffee and talked and talked. He was several years older and he was also married. The affair lasted for four years and has only recently ended. During the whole episode I was married."

The attraction for Barbara was not physical but the fact that the other man was "personable."

"I thought that he was good looking but it was the friendship which developed that I was after. I felt guilty at the very beginning and then it became a part of my life. I saw him as much as possible but it was not a steady every-Tuesday-and-Thursday kind of thing. Our meetings varied. Sometimes we were able to meet on a weekend but it was unusual. During the week I was able to see him because of work. We'd go to hotels together. There's no question that there is a wicked side to it, a naughty side to this kind of thing. But we didn't go to each other's houses, although we lived in adjoining towns. We always met in a city.

"As the relationship grew, I found things about it that were valuable. I was able to discuss things with this man that I couldn't discuss at home. Any subject was okay. While my husband would say, 'You can't do it, it's out of your realm,' my friend would say, 'You can do anything you want to do.' '

Barbara found the beginning of the relationship to be "filled with positive qualities."

"It was like being sixteen again, but this time with knowledge. I felt like a woman of importance, both in and out of bed. I accepted the fact that I had a life, a house, a husband, children and. a job. He was not the cake but the icing and I understood that. In the early days of the affair, I was sleeping with both men and I was able to handle that. I suppose my husband didn't notice that I slept with him less frequently because he was so wrapped up with himself. At the start I think it was a game. Later it became serious. As time went on, I only wanted to be with my lover.

"The sex was excellent. It was very different than with my husband and every time we were together we had sex. I often thought that I would have been willing to explore that kind of sex with my husband if he had been willing but it was out of the question. The sex in the marriage had been adequate until I met this other man. Had I not met him, I wouldn't have known that something better existed. Sex with a married man, like I had, seemed to be about his having had many more women. He knew what to do where I was concerned and he catered to me. As far as AIDS or getting pregnant, I used birth control and I really didn't worry."

She had no difficulty juggling two different lives.

"As long as nothing got mixed together, I was fine. My partner and I understood there were other worlds. We both wanted the same amount from each other, which was to be together with each other whenever we could. My children didn't enter into it at all. They were a part of my other life."

In the end, Barbara's partner decided to pursue a divorce and soon after, he married another woman.

"I was devastated. We had talked about being together. It ended because there was a reason to end it. I don't believe my husband ever found out, and I would have been hurt had he done what I did. Yet I had a need for this or it would not have happened. It wasn't anything that I'd consciously looked for, but it occurred. The fact that it became something more was because I desired it. I'm not sorry that it happened because this partner added to me as a person. I was able to separate my home life from the relationship. Things given to me by my lover actually helped me with my family life. He sort of rounded out what I wasn't getting at home."

When asked if she loved both men at once, Barbara said she did.

"If you have fifteen children you love them, all. Why can't you love all of your men?

"Although he was a terrific lover, I think now that he would make a lousy husband. He was willing to cheat, for starters. If I hadn't been unhappily married, I might not have fallen for him and for the affair.

"My point of view has been changed by the relationship, there's no doubt about that. I see that women are so busy out in the work force that they have no time from age twenty-five to forty to see how they change personally. What you do in your twenties, an age when many women marry, is not necessarily what you'd do or want to do at forty-five. And it applies to marriage. If one marries at twenty-five, by forty-five you have to wonder if this will be the rest of your life. If you marry at thirty-three, you've had more exposure. So for many women who lack the exposure, the affairs work because of the lack of commitment and the lack of substance. They begin as fun and games. And for that very same reason, they don't last. One person in the relationship ends up wanting more; those demands and complications catch up with the affair."

Barbara's story is a bit unusual. Speaking from a mature vantage point, she views an affair as a supplemental relationship, one that makes up for something that has been missed. It sounds as if she was less obsessed with her lover and was capable of coolly assessing him and her husband at the same time. However, it does not sound as if Barbara was intimately involved with either her husband or her lover.

What allowed her to have a more intellectual view of herself and her situation with men was her ability to hold back in each instance. A question of age also arises; when a woman is in her mid-forties it might be a turning point for her. If this turning point exists for some women, then their relationship with men is altered. Barbara's perspective has a different quality to it than that of women in their late thirties or those turning forty.

CRBO

Lisa

Lisa lives in Kentucky, in the same town where she grew up, and is forty-five years old. She has three children and worked full-time while raising them. She describes her childhood and her children's as "filled with love."

"I was twenty-five when I was married. My husband was a man who was unhappy with himself. We moved from house to house in the same town because he was so restless. While we loved each other, it was not always in the right ways. Yet we gave each other the freedom to go out with friends and have a life of our own. I think because my husband was uneducated and I was [educated], it became a problem. He always felt inferior and had to downgrade me to compensate.

"One day I was visiting a friend and I met a man I'd never met before because he was new in town. We were the same age, and he was married. But from the moment we saw each other, there was an attraction. We looked at each other and I thought, this guy is all right.

"For three months he called me and we talked a lot but didn't meet. One night we ran into each other at the movies. I'd gone by myself and he was there with a male friend. We ended up leaving together. We drove on the back roads in the country. We talked and talked and one thing led to another. That was eleven years ago."

Lisa felt there was a "safety valve" in having a relationship with a married man.

"I knew he wouldn't make any demands; there were no obligations. I liked that setup. I didn't want him to leave his wife for me. But I knew his wife didn't like sex and he certainly does. I understood the relationship. His wife was older and he was my age. He didn't have children at the beginning of the affair but during it, he did. I knew she was trying to get pregnant but when it happened I felt very upset. I didn't feel betrayed but I felt very hurt. Yet the fact that I'd had a tubal ligation made it seem especially threatening to me that his wife gave birth. Threatening and sad—it made me feel sad.

"This lover is a very loving and caring person. It was never just for sex like with some men, wild sex without caring. I think that feels good at the time but not afterwards. This was tender sex, a tender relationship. That was why the baby upset me so."

Lisa was able to see her lover on a regular basis, which continued after his child was born.

"We saw each other two times a week. Mostly we went to my house because no one was there during the day. If we drove out of town we'd go to a restaurant or a movie. If we stayed in town, we'd be careful. We always had sex unless he came for a short visit. I never asked him about leaving his wife at any time. I thought maybe he loved her too. I believe that a person can love two people at the same time. I suppose I was in it for the emotional support. He would give me jewelry on special occasions and treated me well, but it was his being there that counted. There were times when I really wanted him to go places with me, which we couldn't do. My sorority party, for instance. I couldn't take him and it was painful to me."

After Lisa's husband died, she began to date other men but no one seemed "special."

"My lover moved to Atlanta and we kept in touch and we saw each other once a month for a while. Now it is down to every other month. After being widowed I realized I had to go ahead with my life and do my thing. I knew I could be without my lover. I was not the type to wait around for him. I'm not that type at all.

"Some women I've seen will wait for their lovers to call but I knew I had to move forward. I think of all the times I shared with my lovers. Several times we were able to get away together. We'd go to the mountains to take little vacations and they were wonderful special days. I think of them and I wonder about the future. I don't know if my lover fits into my scheme. I don't think I want a permanent relationship or another marriage, but I'm not sure.

"I have witnessed some lousy situations with men but I realize there are some nice men out there too. You have to open yourself up and take a chance. I'm not sure I want to do that. My lover protected me from having to face that decision."

Lisa is ready to leave her lover because she wants the security of knowing "someone will be there."

"I'm ready to go because I want to be with someone I can be seen with, someone to grow old with and rock on my porch with. If I had known how emotionally involved I'd become I think I would have avoided the whole thing. It was too deep and draining. Maybe I was obsessed with him at some point but I never recognized it at the time. We had a very comfortable relationship. We're still best friends. But in its day, it was a marriage of its own. That was something else."

It sounds as if Lisa loved this man but was disillusioned with the relationship. She was unable to see him on her terms and finally she realized that she wanted more than he was able to offer. The fact that Lisa was widowed and free to do as she pleased altered her thinking. When her lover moved out of town it provided her with a natural break in the relationship. Although she suffered in certain ways–for example, when her lover's wife gave birth and when he could not be with her–she also enjoyed the aspects of the tryst that worked for her.

Lisa's attachment showed her what kind of relationship would suit her needs. She's taking that valuable information to the next man, hoping it will work for her.

Conclusion

⚘

When I wrote the introduction to this book, I had conducted ten interviews. I began the project based on perception, intuition and a general sense of what I expected to hear and thought that I knew. Having encountered scores of actual tales in the hundreds of hours I put into this project, I realize I was largely unprepared for the intensity and diversity of the phenomenon of married women and their romances.

In many cases I was informed of secrets, deeply buried truths. I believe that I offered an opportunity for each woman to speak for as long as she wished, in as much detail as she chose, about her, lover or lovers. While essentially the life span of my connection to each woman was limited to the length of the interview itself, a link formed and a bond arose. I listened without judgment, hoping that it was cathartic to some degree and that, at the same time, it would provide a support system for the untold others who envision their own versions.

With rare exceptions, I felt sucked into the vortex of these women's lives and heard something extreme in their words and attitudes, something purged and honest. What I am left with is an almost overwhelming sense of the fundamental validity of what affairs in today's world offer to women. Though each voice was distinct, their collective message is clear and unsettling. These unfaithful wives, in their yearning and calculation, lust and uncertainty, are indistinguishable from the rest of us, except for their willingness to act upon their passion. I was left with an ineffable sense that their actions, far from neurotic or extreme, were both healthy and alarmingly rational.

These liaisons with lovers in the course of a marriage are not new, as I've said before; yet there is an aspect to these affairs that differentiates them from extramarital relationships in the past. While of course each has its own individual circumstances, many are socially driven. It is this aspect, the affair as a by-product of the permanently changed role of the wife in American society, that impresses me as most significant.

CRED

Women of today, as a result of the women's movement as well as the dynamic of women in the workplace, have a heightened self-awareness. Their exposure to men, their access to men, is different than in the past. The role and gender of the provider have been altered, bringing about changes in the nuclear family. A sense of entitlement prevails, touching not only educated, upper-class women as the initial women's movement of the sixties did, but filtering to women of various walks of life, race, and social strata.

The affairs conducted by married women of today in this country take place within a fundamentally modified environment which causes and enables women to interact with men. The woman of the new millennium, with her flexibility and mobility, has consciously reached out for the option of enhanced sexuality. From the interviews it appears that few women seem unhappy to be having these trysts. Instead they welcome a situation which can be explored; the consequences seem to be of less concern than the chance to enter the experience. And because of the strong networking of the contemporary woman, she has the ability to discuss her actions, which she views as valuable in terms of self-growth. This is not a matter of philosophy but a matter of influence; being exposed to many opportunities, and to many social messages that prize romance above all, they eventually and yield and are catapulted into another universe.

These stories are not aberrations, nor are they a group of isolated infidelities. Rather, they are a surging American voice, an inextricable and exponentially expanding component of the wife as not simply homemaker and mother but as equally educated, equally responsible provider. The external manifestation of this change, expressed through women's liberation and the feminist movement, generally has only attracted a moderate following. Words and symbols are often difficult to agree with, but deeds and desires are not. In these interviews I have witnessed not a sense of admission but a sense of just deserts.

ৎৎ৵০

The "passion for more" which American wives see today is a part of our culture, not a reaction against it. It is something that will become a greater and more common aspect of modern life. Many people do not vote at the ballot box, but vote with their feet. While the anatomy in question may differ, this is the vote that American wives are making today–for meaningful sexual freedom consistent with their more prominent role in society.

I now recognize the choices available to women in America. I see that one solution is to explore outside the traditional boundaries. So many of us have accepted the alleged rules in a marriage. Yet more and more are breaking the rules, going outside the lines to achieve what cannot be achieved within those restrictions. Beyond the barrier stands the lover, and women today cross the line readily, in search of affirmation, sex, freedom, self, and love.